Mr. Olympia

Mr. Universe

Mr. America

Mr. World

Mr. Olympus

Mr. Championship

Jr. Mr. America

Mr. International

Mr. Galaxy

Mr. Pro World Cup

Mr. Chicago

Mr. Long Beach

Mr. Azteca Int'

Mr. Illinois

Sergio Oliva
The Myth

Sergio Oliva

with Frank Marchante

Sergio Oliva the Myth, Building the Ultimate Physique

Published by Gras Publishing Company
Miami, Florida

Website: www.SergioOlivaTheMyth.com

 Editor /Production Manager: Gilda Marchante
Cover: Frank Marchante

Library of Congress Control: 2006924450

Library of Congress Cataloging-in-Publication Data
Marchante, Frank
Sergio Oliva the Myth, Building the Ultimate Physique
P. 350
ISBN-0-9779040-1-6
ISBN-978-0-9779040-1-3

1. Bodybuilding/Weight Training- Handbook-Manuals 2.Fitness 3. Health
4. Sport and Recreation 5. Weight Loss
 United States -Biography.
613.8'5-dc22

This book was printed on acid-free paper

Acknowledgements

I would like to thank all the bodybuilders, fitness models and photographers who contributed with photographs for this book. Including Casey Viator, Arthur Jones, Lisa Brewer, Grace Rivera, Frank Zane, Lou Ferrigno, Jay Cutler, Shawn Ray, Tony Lanza, Russ Wagner, Robby Robinson, Ed Corney, Frank Marchante Jr., Wayne Gallash, Dave Draper, Ben Kamata of Bodybuilding Magazine Japan, Bolshakova Irina Aka Schnneeflocke, David Landau, Amy Fadhli, George Legeros, Jamneth Cordoba, George Helmer of Steve Reeves International, Dr. Christian Anderson of Sandow museum, Flex Wheeler, Richard Morris, Art Zeller, Yules, Dennis Weis, Lee Labrada , Gilda Marchante and Michelle Marchante.

Many thanks to Jack Merjimekian for his pictures. A special thanks to Denie, a fantastic, most talented photographer/editor whom so generously donated his time/talent and gave me so many awesome pictures for the creation of this book. Finally I want to thank Robert Kennedy of MuscleMag International, always ready to reach out and help both old timers and new. When we asked him to write the Foreword for this book he gladly accepted without hesitation. He also gave us many pictures for the book. All of which we are all very grateful for. Thanks to all.

Photo by Denie.

FOREWORD

By Robert Kennedy

Anyone who loves the sport of bodybuilding knows the name of Sergio Oliva, known as "The Myth". I greatly admired him and consider him to be the all-time world's greatest physique. I saw him in competition many times, including his shows against Arnold. There is no doubt that with his wide shoulders and narrow hip structure he was superior to any other bodybuilder of his generation. Sergio was not only the most aesthetic bodybuilder on stage but also the biggest. In addition to his extraordinary physique, his special charisma would excite the audience into a frenzy of adoring fans. Few men could claim as much.

He trained in his own way and knew exactly how he wanted to look. Sergio Oliva is considered by most to be the world's most genetically gifted bodybuilder. With his privileged genetics he acquired an incredible physique that would inspire millions. It is a fact that Sergio Oliva's body made an impact in the world of bodybuilding forever. He set a whole new standard for competitive bodybuilding; loved by millions, revered by many, and feared by some. He was so huge and extremely proportioned that he used to bring chills to his adversaries. This is how he acquired the name of "The Myth".

Sergio Oliva's competitions were always heavily anticipated and full of electricity, many ending with controversial decisions, adding to the legend. At the time Sergio became involved with bodybuilding, civil right issues were very intense in the United States, and thus reaching championship status was very difficult. However, against all odds, he was the first black athlete to win the IFBB Mr. America, Mr. World, Mr. Universe and Mr. Olympia titles. He won the Mr. Olympia three times, in 1967, 1968, and 1969. In fact, in 1968 Sergio made history when he won that title uncontested. Since then, history has never been able to repeat itself.

Now Sergio has written his memoirs, representing the Golden Era of bodybuilding. Some of the chapters in this book are about Sergio's childhood, how he developed his amazing physique, his thoughts about competition, posing, supplements, steroids, and nutrition. He also gets into the specifics of training individual body parts to obtain maximum results and much more. Sergio's long awaited first book is definitely overdue and a must have for bodybuilding enthusiasts. He's a genuine champion of the sport and one of its greatest legends.

Robert Kennedy
Editor and Publisher
MuscleMag International

Quotes about Sergio

"Sergio's long awaited book is definitely overdue and a must have for bodybuilding enthusiasts".
Robert Kennedy-Editor-Publisher-MuscleMag International

"Sergio is truly the embodiment of THE MYTH". Sergio Oliva is to bodybuilding what Babe Ruth is to baseball. Few bodybuilders have transcended time and have captured the imagination of generations of fans in the manner in which Sergio has. Sergio is a living legend.
Lee Labrada -Mr. Universe- Night of champion- winner- Founder-Ceo Labrada Nutrition

"Sergio was maybe the greatest bodybuilder ever, a complete package of mass, symmetry, and definition, which are the tools to be the best".
 "A true legend and a great champion".
Jay Cutler- Arnold S Classic-Night of Champions- winner- Mr. Olympia

"Sergio was by far one of the pioneers of bodybuilding. When I got started he was an inspiration of another kind! Size, strength and proportion were the adjectives I used to describe the ultimate physique.
When you look in the dictionary under the word bodybuilder, there should be a photo of Sergio".
"He definitely had an impact on my decision to pursue the sport of bodybuilding!"
Shawn Ray – Arnold S Classic- national- winner- Mr. Olympia 2nd

"The largest muscular arm that I ever measured or saw was Sergio Oliva which accurately measured "cold" 20 1/8 inches. He was as lean as a well-conditioned racehorse".
Arthur Jones -Founder -CEO-owner Nautilus machine-Author- Trainer Expert

"I have seen all the pros in bodybuilding through the years, and no one can match his size and density.
I met him at the age of 19 years old, I was struck by his genetics instantly, small waist, wide shoulders, and calves that could match anyone's even today.
We trained together in Florida for a while, and he was always an inspiration to me.
He makes you want to get busy training, I felt like I was always behind in my training around Sergio, he was so freaking huge.
The man doesn't have an ego, he helped me with training and diet in my early years, there is a bunch of great information in this man's head.
This book we'll be a great success for years to come.
I'm proud to call Sergio Oliva one of my closest friends".
Casey Viator Mr.USA -Mr. America -Mr. Universe

"Sergio was so far advanced over the rest of us. He was phenomenal, and he had certain characteristics that I personally believe have never been equaled by anyone ever.
When you saw the guy, he was awesome, it's like you couldn't take it at all. You couldn't believe this guy was truly a human being. He was certainly 20 years too early; he could compete with the top guys of today and probably be better than they are. Sergio was the best".
Boyer Coe Mr. Universe- Mr. America

"Sergio was just a different kind of human being than I had seen before. Sergio has always been a very friendly guy and a real gentleman. He never did any of those tricks on stage that we see so often now. You could compete with him and congratulate him and feel congratulated by him if you won".
Larry Scott Mr. Olympia-Mr. America-Mr. universe

"Sergio had one of the greatest physiques in the story of bodybuilding and inspired me tremendously in the late 60's".
Frank Zane Mr. Olympia -Mr. Universe -Mr. America

"He was tremendous; he had more muscle, more thickness than anybody, very well proportioned".
Steve Reeves Mr. Universe – Mr. America

"He was terrific, very wide shoulders, very slim midsection, and his muscle mass so unusual that you could call it phenomenal".
John Grimek Mr.America-Mr.Universe-Mr.USA

"Most people refer to Sergio Oliva as one of bodybuilding's greatest all time champions... they are wrong, he's more than that".
Denie – Writer-Editor-Photographer

"Sergio Oliva literally broke the mold, and he broke it in more than one place. One might say he broke the whole darn thing .Who really looked like this creature for basic power, muscle size and density, hardness and symmetry? Was he another species of animal not yet categorized? He revealed and displayed more than anyone before and anyone since a primitive muscular completeness... and carriage of grace to belie the brute-ness".
Dave Draper-Mr. America- Mr. Universe- Mr. World

"Sergio was so huge he could beat you in the dressing room if you weren't careful. His shirt would come off, and there would be that incredible mass. He would transfix you with a look, exhale with a kind of animal grunt, and suddenly the lats would begin to flare..... And just when you thought they were the most unbelievable lats ...you ever saw, bom-out they would come more and more, until you began to doubt that this was a human being you were looking at".
Arnold Schwarzenegger- Mr. Olympia-Mr. Universe- Mr. World

"Sergio was one of the few bodybuilders that had ever inspired me besides Arnold Schwarznegger. Pound for pound Sergio was one of the greatest bodybuilders of all time due to his muscle shape, muscle insertions, small waist line, he carried more mass than any bodybuilder that I have ever seen, even according to today's standard! Sergio was a bodybuilder that was complete, great abs, great arms, great legs, overall great balanced physique. In today's physique, where guys are bigger and better than me, in his prime, Sergio can be included in the top of this group easily".
Danny Padilla -Mr. America Mr. Universe

"The first bodybuilding contest I attended was in 1976. Sergio Oliva was a guest poser. My jaw dropped when I saw his incredible size and thickness. He looked bigger than humanly possible".
John Hansen. Mr. Natural Universe – Mr. Natural Olympia

"I know Sergio Oliva's book is going to be a great success".
Ed Courney. Mr. America-Mr.Universe-Mr. World

"When I first saw pictures of Sergio Oliva at the 1967 Mr. Olympia, I was amazed! I didn't think was possible for a man to look like that-to build his body to that extreme. Immediately I fell in love with bodybuilding and wanted to go for it from that point on".
Robby Robinson Mr. Universe- Mr. America- Mr. World

"Sergio was the ultimate freak, not ugly but beautiful. His physique was compatible with today guys, like Ronnie Coleman".
Mike Katz Mr. America-1970

"Sergio is one of the best built men to ever have walked this Earth and I'm proud to have known him... Sergio the man, Sergio the champion, but most of all Sergio the gregarious, humorous, and entertaining gentleman".
Denie – Writer-Editor-Photographer

"Everybody I knew thought that when he was beaten by Arnold Scharzenegger in Essen Germany, that was a farce"
"Sergio was the first bodybuilder with the first freaky muscle size".
George Turner -Training expert

"Sergio Oliva literally cracked the cement in the auditorium (guest posing at the Mr. Universe 1978) when he showed how the world's best developed man should look. To me, he is the greatest; I have seen and been around for a while". **Dick Taylor- Photographer- Writer**

And so we go... Greeks had Hercules... contemporary bodybuilding has Sergio!
Denie Writer-Editor-Photographer

"Sergio Oliva was the greatest, yes, Arnold was also competing, but Sergio was the man".
Reb's Orrell Politically Sport Archives

DEDICATION

I would like to dedicate this book to my son, Sergio, and daughter Julie whom I love with all my heart and make my life worth living.

To my mother, you were always an inspiration to me and you will always live in my memory and heart. You taught me never to be afraid and to go after what I wanted in life. You taught me well.

Sergio Oliva

To my mother and father: I always told you I would write Sergio Oliva's book. I hope that you can see it from the heavens above. Thanks to my son, Frank for helping out with all the photo shoots and a special thanks to my wife, Gilda, who dedicated endless hours to this project. I could have never done this book without her. To my daughter, Monica, for giving me wonderful grandchildren and to my daughter Michelle for always being there inspiring me and whose love for books rivals my own. Last but not least, my companion on those lonely, long hours in the middle of the night, my beautiful little dog Toby.

Frank Marchante

INTRODUCTION

The late 60's, was a turbulent time in the United States and around the world. I was a young skinny guy, walking home from school, when suddenly, it happened. I saw Sergio Oliva in a magazine cover at a newsstand, without hesitation I bought the magazine. The man in the picture was humongous; with perfect proportions, long muscles, and incredible symmetry. From that moment on I wanted to train and look like him. The way he inspired me, he inspired thousands of others. That is how I met Sergio Oliva.

Sergio possessed the most superior, favorable genetics of all bodybuilders. He won many major competitions. They called him THE MYTH, and he certainly lived up to those attributes. Oliva's name was heard in chants when colossal men competed against each other. "Sergio, Sergio, Sergio!", the fans screamed as they waited for the 27- inch waist, 58- inch chest, and 22- inch arms superhero spread his back like a black cobra ready to attack. Sergio has lived his life like the song "My Way", "His Way", without compromising one single value. He always stood tall for the truth he believed in no matter the price he had to pay.

In 1967 Oliva captured top honors in the Mr. Universe in front of 10,000 screaming fans at the World's Fair in Montreal and the Mr. Olympia, the World Series of Muscles , at the Brooklyn Academy of Music. The following year Oliva won again but the Myth was all alone. No competitors were willing to risk looking scrawny in his shadow.

Sergio's long awaited book is full of wisdom and knowledge. How did Oliva ever develop the most outstanding body ever created? When God made Sergio, he broke the mold. No one has ever been built like Sergio and probably no one ever will. His workouts were extremely hard together with a super strong determination to be the best. He had a God like mysterious way to recuperate from heavy training to become the best of the best to accomplish this goal. On stage he had an extreme magnetism and animal elegance that left people shouting for him. I am delighted, proud, and honored to have been part of this book.

Frank Marchante

Miami, Fl

DISCLAIMER PAGE

Warning

Before starting any exercise program see your doctor and ask for a complete physical exam, including a stress test. Especially if you have never exercised, are pregnant, or suffer from any illnesses. As with all exercise and dietary programs, you should get your doctor's approval before beginning. Always read and follow safety instructions.

The exercise and dietary programs in this book are not intended as a substitute for any exercise program or dietary regimen that may have been prescribed by your doctor.

The purpose of this manual is to educate and entertain. The author, Publisher and Sergio Oliva should have neither liability nor responsibility to any person or entity with respect to any loss or damaged caused, or allege to be caused, directly or indirectly by the information contained in this book.

This manual is as accurate as possible. However there may be mistakes both typographical and in content. Therefore it should be used only as a guide and not as the ultimate source. This book contains Sergio Oliva's personal opinions as told to Francisco Marchante.

A NOTE FROM SERGIO

In my opinion a fitness book wouldn't be complete if it does not get into important topics such as diabetes, blood pressure, arthritis, teeth and feet, among others. These are topics that I don't see in any other fitness book. The human body is like a chain, so what good is it if one part is weak? That is why I tried to make this book as detailed and complete as possible.

For years I've wanted to sit down and write a book, to tell the whole world my life story, victories, and defeats. However, it always seemed like I never could find the time to do it. Finally I sat and wrote my thoughts, memories, and life experiences. It was not an easy task to do, but I did it.

– Sergio Oliva

SAFETY INSTRUCTIONS

   If at any time you feel pain, light headed or dizziness, stop exercising immediately! Follow your doctor's recommendations and know your limits when training. Use common sense when exercising.

Get a Physical

The first thing you should do before starting any exercise program is to have your doctor give you a check-up. A complete physical including a stress test is a good idea and when you get a clean bill of health from your physician start slowly. Take your time. It took you years to get out of shape so don't try to get in shape in a hurry. Warning symptoms to keep in mind are:

1. Chest pain

2. Dizziness

3. Fainting

4. Stomach pain

If you have any of these problems, please, consult your doctor before training.

1. High blood pressure

2. History of heart disease

3. High cholesterol

4. Obesity

5. Sedentary live

If at any time you feel bad stop right away!

Call your doctor and have him look into the problem.

Contents

Colossal mass and incredible muscularity-awesome

Chapter 1
A Champion Is Born

    I was born on July 4th, 1939, in Havana, Cuba, the largest island of the Caribbean between the Caribbean Sea and the North Atlantic Ocean, just south of Florida. I lived on 5th Street and Martín Pérez in Guanabacoa, one of the oldest districts of Havana. The name Guanabacoa comes from the Cuban Indians the Tainos and it means water place. The aroma of bread from the bakeries blended together with the smell of freshly brewed Cuban coffee, along with the sound of beating drums were always lingering throughout the town.

    The Spanish roots and African roots came together to create a real Caribbean atmosphere. The African slaves that were shipped to Cuba brought many rhythms that blended with Spanish music. The famous Afro-Cuban music and dance the Guaguanco was developed in the streets of Guanabacoa, Havana. The Conga is said to be developed by the slaves. Other kinds of music are said to be derived from this rhythm as well. There were small opened areas; green lawn parks with metal benches, three beautiful churches were located there: Nuestra Señora de la Asunción, El Convento de Santo Domingo and the Church of San Francisco. There was also a famous natural water company, La Cotorra.

    There were people always walking around, Havana Solar, and ancient mansions too. The world famous Cuban composer, conductor, and pianist, Ernesto Lecuona, was also born in Guanabacoa. I lived in Guanabacoa until I left Cuba.

Sergio's Neighborhood

My father's name was Francisco but they called him Pancho. He was a strong man; he used to work 7 days a week Monday through Friday as a plumber, Saturday and Sunday as a street vendor. I remember he had a good friendly personality. My mother's name was Julia. Oh, What a Woman! She was stronger than my dad. She was, big, smart, and yes, I remember her with a smile always on her face and a song on her lips, always dancing. My mother was a hard worker; she took care of all 20 of us and hand washed laundry for other people to help out my father with a little extra cash. She was an inspiration in my life. Unfortunately, they have both passed away.

I have 11 brothers and 9 sisters from both sides of my parents. Sadly two of them passed away.

As a young boy I remember being very happy. I was mischievous, not too bad but very playful. For some reason I only remember one of my teacher's name, Conchita. As you can imagine having such a big family, the economy not very stable, and the Revolution taking place it wasn't easy. Our family encountered great struggles. However, like in any family or situation, we had good times and bad times.

As I grew older, I was kind of skinny but very strong. I began working very hard when I was young. At 13 years of age, I was working, buying my own clothes and basically supporting myself. I also would give money to my mother to help her out financially.

I built a wheelbarrow so that I could go around and collect chicken bones and beef bones and sell them to factories that utilized them for processing. Sometimes I use to also pick up old newspapers around El Barrio Obrero, an upper class neighborhood and sell them to the butcher shops for beef wrapping. When there were no bones or newspapers to pick up I use to collect glass bottles in other upper class neighborhoods. As you can imagine this was very hard work for me to do, especially in the summer months when the tropical sun was so hot and I walked miles and miles pushing that wheel barrow, after a while, it got really heavy.

At that time, markets and bottle factories use to give money for the glass bottles. I remember well buying a Pepsi or Coca Cola and leaving a 2 or 3 cents deposit. But I was making good money, I was buying my personal things and I had money left over to help my mother. At 13 it was very hard for me to work all the time when other kids my age were playing and having fun. But I did it. I had to work. My family was very low income and that's the way it was.

This made the foundation for my later years to be able to develop my body. I had a good personality, I was a good dancer, I could dance anything, salsa, rumba, merengue. I laughed a lot and went dancing a lot. We use to walk around or sit in Guanabacoa's park, talk among friends and watched the young, beautiful Cuban girls walk by. We were happy if we just got a glimpse or a smile from them.

I use to go to The Tropical (one of Cuba's best beer brewery) grounds, where they use to have huge parties. There's one particular day that I have never forgotten. I was dressed with a white Guayabera (typical Cuban shirt) and had money for only a one-way trip for the bus and a couple of pesos for a Coke or a beer. I met a white beautiful young girl; we liked each other and danced all night long. We could have spent the night together but I did not have any money for a room. So we had to say goodbye. Coño!

To go home, I had to wait for a bus to come by and when it drove off, I hung myself from the back bumper all the way home. Young kids used this method to travel sometimes. To this day I regret not being able to spend the night with that beautiful young girl.

I would also attend El Carnaval held once a year in the Habana, Malecon where beautiful women paraded in beautiful floats. There were all kinds of music, pachanga, conga, etc., foods like pan con lechon (pork sandwich), lemonade, soda, and beer.

El Carnaval lasted a whole week, people dressed in different kinds of costumes. The comparsa, where people took to the streets and danced La Conga (African-Latin music), in the streets of the Malecon.

The beautiful costumes, the music, the food all made Cuba's Carnaval one of the most famous in the world. Only second, I believe, to the one in Rio, Brazil.

Here you had the opportunity of making new friends and meeting tourist and of course, beautiful women. Opportunities I didn't take lightly.

Every neighbor in Cuba had his own comparsa (dancing team) and competed against each other dancing, beautiful clothes, and ingenuity. Here after dancing, eating, drinking and after the Carnaval that ran late into the night was over, you would walk down the Malecon (famous sidewalk by the ocean in Havana) with your girlfriend talking or looking for a dark spot to kiss or find a cheap room where to spend the night. It was magic those crazy nights in Cuba and I took part in all of them. I participated every weekend in the brewery grounds party, and also in the beautiful huge parties they use to have in front of the Capitol (every weekend with the women orchestra famous at the time). I also participated in the Carnival every year.

What memories those days were, tropical rhythm, heat, beautiful women, perfume in the air, and crazy fast nights in Havana. I was young and always looking for fun it made me feel alive and well! This was the time when all the people in Cuba got together to dance, enjoy, and have a real good time, no matter the color of your skin, religion, or background. The exuberant friendliness of the Cuban people shone through. The buses were so full you couldn't take any. It was almost impossible to walk the streets. The smell of the ocean mixed with the smell of food, the beat of the music in your ear, and the sight of beautiful and provocative women all around made the Carnaval the ultimate party. This is where I was born, Cuba, a tropical island in the Carribean. However, all of this came to an end when communism took over.

Havana, Cuba

Looking back now I can say that I always had a small waist. If I remember correctly my entire family also had a small waist. I have to thank both my parents for the genes they passed on to me. I thank them for my physical attributes and my mother for her guidance.

I was not what you can call an athletic young boy, but thinking back I always had a small waist. I remember looking at the mirror as a kid and noticing my shoulders were bigger than my waist. By the age of 15 I was enrolled in the Cuban Army prior to Castro's regime. The people that enrolled me, had to lie about my age because I was suppose to be 18 years old to enroll.

One of my unforgettable memories from the Army was when we were walking through the mountain jungles of Saguadetanamo, Oriente for days looking for rebels. We had no commodities, no good food, not even an adequate place to sleep or rest. Then all of a sudden I saw a blurred figure come out of the jungle. We looked at each other for a split of a second. This figure had shoulder length hair, for a moment I was confused, and I thought it was a woman. So, I put my Garan rifle down but it was not a woman, instead it was a guerilla man. Who in turned raised his rifle in a split of a second and shot me in my right arm. But not before I got a glimpse of him running away with a damn long beard, the size of all of Guanabacoa! To this day, I can still see him running into the jungle.

I was rushed to the doctor who told me that I would probably never be able to use my right arm again. Wrong! Thanks to my constitution, determination, and of course the blessing of Cachita, the patron of Cuba, Virgen del Cobre. I am Catholic and a great follower of the patron of Cuba, La Caridad del Cobre. As a matter of fact, the big medallion that hangs in my chest symbolizes her and it was a gift from my mother. I never take it off and it means a lot to me.

La Caridad, Church, Miami, FL

Now I would like to tell you about something that I was not going to include in the book but people that know me said I just had to. One day I was running trying to catch the bus, when all of a sudden a Volkswagen hit me and believe it or not, I dented the bumper to my surprise, nothing happen to me except for the scare of the moment. However the Volkswagen owner couldn't say the same thing. The driver and the people that witness the accident couldn't believe it either.

Later on, the Cuban Revolution prevailed and Fidel Castro led the rebels with long hair to power. His iron will has always controlled the country since then. A Communist Revolution, where by the way, bodybuilding at the time was prohibited like in Russia. A place where you have to work all day, 8 to 10 hours a day and on Saturdays and Sundays you have to go to the sugar mills to cut sugar cane supposedly "voluntarily" and at night you have to be on guard to look over the neighborhood. The government tells you what to do, when, and how to think. But I personally could not handle having people telling me what to do, when to do it and how to do it. I am a rebel! I don't like people controlling my life.

So I decided I had to leave the country. I could not live there anymore. But how would I leave?
That was the question that kept taunting my mind, over and over again "How"? Some of my friends called me and told me they were going to escape in a raft. They invited me to go with them, more than once, maybe three or four times. "Damn Sergio!" "Come with us"!
"We built a small raft made out of some old car tire tubes and some wood and we are ready to leave Cuba tonight"!
"We will leave through El Malecón from La Havana".

One time I said, "Carajo, yes!" but at the last moment I backed out because the truth was, I was scared to be eaten by a shark or die drowning. I told myself, —Sergio this is not the right way for you. You have to find another way. I think it's crazy the way the Cuban people risked their lives, and most still do, with those rafts made out of tubes and ropes.

Finally one day I realized that if I joined a sports team that would be my ticket out of Cuba. I remember trying boxing but "shit" those hits were hard, carajo! Then I tried track and field, but I came from a poor family and with the revolution in effect, food was very scarce and I could not keep up with all the well fed, better off competitors from the Vedado, a classy neighborhood in Cuba (at that time).

Then I tried to play baseball, softball, tennis, swimming but nothing was made for me or me for it. Then one day I saw a group of very strong men at the beach, I was looking at them and they were looking at me. My physique was strong but skinny; we got together and talked for a while. One of the guys in the group told me they were weightlifters and invited me to go to the gym. The gym's name was the Roger Gonzalez Gym. It was located at Marcell and Versailles Street, Guanabacoa. In the gym he told me.
"You are built to be a champion"!
"If you clean the gym and help us, you can train with us, and maybe you can join the weight lifting team".

The first time I picked up a barbell I knew I had found my thing in life. That's how I got into the Cuban weight lifting team. I was the middle heavy weight, 198 pounds, and my brother was the heavy weight. On the three lifts, clean, jerk, and snatch, I lifted 1000 pounds. My brother who was bigger and stronger than me lifted 1050 pounds, I was 18 years old then and my brother was 21 years old.

We started to train to see if we could get into the Pan American Cuban Team. I cleaned, helped around, did anything that had to be done, moved things and in exchange they would help me train. My brother and I made the team but in the meantime Cuba's political situation was getting worse. There was less food, no work, everything was very scarce, less freedom every passing day. The communist's propaganda was that an invasion of the island was imminent. People were lining up for hours to get whatever little food they could find. There was no bread, no milk. I was getting more and more desperate living in Cuba and on top of it all, that "voluntary" work of cutting sugar cane over the weekend with no pay, and guarding the streets at night, left no time for me to enjoy life. It was very frustrating to say the least.

Young Sergio in Cuba – Courtesy Frank Marchante

Little by little, we were being trained for the Pan American Games that were going to be held in Jamaica. It was proposed that the team be sent to Russia for three months so that we may be professionally trained for the games.

This created another dilemma for the Oliva brothers. My brother, who was older than I, did not want to go. He was afraid that if Cuba was invaded and the government was overthrown maybe we would be stuck in Russia forever, faraway from our family without being able to come back to our family or our country. Sadly he didn't go but in reality, he was a great champion and he probably would have won the First Place Gold Medal in the Pan American Games in Jamaica. What a waste, things could have been different for him.

I remember the trip to Russia was very long and very tiring. We took off from Jose Marti International Airport and landed at Moscow Airport. The trip seemed to last forever. I remember working very hard in Russia. The training was very strenuous and intense. By then I was much, much stronger, and muscular. I can honestly say that the base of my body was built, in combination with all the hard work done in Cuba for years and this heavy training it was evident. The beginning of the champion of bodybuilding, Sergio Oliva was born. My back, chest, shoulders, arms, and legs were full. I was much bigger, weighed more; I was not that skinny young kid anymore. I was turning into the shadow of what was to come years later.

Russia was cold and overcastted most of the time. Its people in my opinion were not friendly or open. They looked at foreigners with suspicion. They also drank too much. As a matter of fact, they drank most of the time. Of course, in every country you find all kinds of people. Keep in mind that my trip was during the 60's under communist Russia. Probably things have changed by now. They probably dress better now and maybe they are happier or friendlier.

During my visit I missed the Cuban food a lot. I also missed my family, especially my mother. When it was time to return to Cuba, I was excited and happy to go back and embrace my mother again. The trip was long and tiring but I was happy to land in Cuba. My trip to Russia was quite an experience.

Courtesy: Dennis Weis

An incident that comes to mind is when the entire Cuban team went to the Red Square in Moscow and we saw a long line of Russian people and tourist. We found out they were there waiting for hours to see the mummy of Lenin. I told the team, (I was the captain of the Cuban team), "I am not going to spend two or three hours in line just to see a mummy."

Months later, when we went back to Cuba, and we got to the villas we used to live in, Fidel Castro paid us a surprise visit. El Caballo, (The Horse) as we called him in Cuba walked over to me with a cigar in his lips, placed his hand over my shoulder and said:

"¡Oye, tu eres la candela!" (Hey, you are something else!)

And with that he said:

"I am not going to make a line and spend two or three hours just to see a mummy."

I was shocked; these were the exact words I said in Russia. The same words I had said to the team. I was certain that nobody in the team had said anything, or was I; especially since I was with them, all of the time. When we arrived to Cuba we went from the airport straight to the villas. Therefore the only possible explanation was that Fidel had a spy among us, or one of the Russians spoke Spanish and we did not know it.

Anyway I got chills, my blood froze like an iceberg, and I thought it was the end for me. For a moment I thought he was going to screw me over and send me to jail or worse.

One word from Castro's lips could mean your life is over. You could be sent to jail for 10 to 20 years in a split of a second, or to a firing squad. Fortunately, nothing happened, he turned around and gave us one of those long tiring speeches about us being the best team in the whole world and how the Cuban reputation lied over our shoulders and he went on and on. Suddenly, just as quickly as he came in, he left in a flash.

Early 20's

When I think about that moment I still feel a chill in my body. You have to keep in mind that I just wanted to be in the team so that I could escape Cuba. It was my way to freedom. At that moment in time, I remember thinking:

Does he know?

Does he suspect anything?

Are they aware?

Do they have somebody just spying on me?

Many different and crazy thoughts went through my mind at that moment. It was one of those times that I would never forget.

From that moment on I was more cautious. I kept my eyes and ears opened at all times and watch my steps carefully. I learned my lesson the hard way. I watched my steps and kept my thoughts to myself, especially, the ones about freedom. Now more than ever, it was just a matter of time. I just had to wait my time would come.

Sergio's incredible back and delts, even at a young age

Leap to Freedom

Kingston, Jamaica

Days before my escape (1961) I was very anxious. I was trying to locate the U.S. Embassy and of course I had to be really careful. We had Castro's secret police traveling with us, and also spies were among us. The Russian incident was still very present in my mind.

Every time we went out, I looked and looked for the embassy, and I could not ask anyone where it was because spying eyes were watching all the time. I felt jailed even though I was not in a cell. I could not speak or move freely. I wanted to be a free man, make my own choices, have my own thoughts, and my own actions.

Then I saw it. It was like seeing an oasis in the middle of the dessert, but the way it happened was kind of funny. I saw a man selling mangos with a wheelbarrow and I love mangos. So I approached him and when I was buying the mangos I looked up and there it was, the American flag, with its bright stripes and shining stars. Simply beautiful, and at that moment, I found it even more beautiful. But I had to control myself so that I wouldn't just take off running for it. My breath got heavier, but I was surrounded by Cuban Officials, I was afraid I was going to get caught. I told myself, "Sergio wait. Wait Sergio!"

As I was going back to the hotel, I made a road map in my head. I paid close attention to

Old Glory – What a Sight to See

the streets I took, turns I made, and any other minor detail I may have noticed. I was afraid and worried that I would never have another chance.

When I got back to the hotel, I found out that the Cuban officials were departing its people back to Cuba right after the competition. The entire Cuban team was at the hotel. I said, "Shit my competition is tomorrow. I have to do it now, today!"

I said, "The hell with it. It's now or never"! I knew that if I stayed and competed the next day I would be taking the chance to be sent back to Cuba right after the competition missing the opportunity of a lifetime. So I told myself then and there, "No way Sergio, do it, do it now!"

I turned around and aimed straight for the door. I left walking without saying a word or taking anything with me. No clothes, no money, nothing! I remember my heart pumping fast, my breath was deep and agitated. I was risking thirty years in jail or the firing squad.

I was wearing a pair of shorts, no shoes, and a cap. I walked. Walked fast! Taking the same streets I had recorded in my mind not so long ago.

Behind me I could hear voices and people yelling.
"Hey Sergio wait! Sergio where are you going?"
I paid no attention and kept walking and I mean fast! By now, I was doing what you call nowadays brisk walking. I finally turned the last corner, and there it was the American embassy with the American flag swaying in the air like saluting me. One block was all that was between freedom, communism, or jail.

Bohemia – Cuba magazine   *Sergio- WeightLifting Cuba Champion*

I looked back and all of a sudden I saw about ten people running my way. I recognized some of them as Castro's secret police. I began to run as fast as I could, as I got closer to the US embassy I also saw a bunch of Jamaican police officers running towards me left and right. I told myself at that instant, "No one, but no one, is going to stop me from getting my freedom". As I approached the embassy the people behind me were also closing in on me. So were the Jamaican police officers and the Cuban police. I was cornered, trapped, with no way to reach the embassy. So I jumped over the wheelbarrow filled with mangos, reached over the fence, climbed and jumped to the other side. Once I jumped and turned around I couldn't believe my eyes. The Cuban athletes and the Cuban Secret Police were not chasing me; they were all running to get their freedom as well. They were all defecting. "My god, this is incredible!" I thought. Unbelievable even the Secret Police was jumping over the fence. One guy even threw a bag over the fence before he jumped. We were eighteen in all.

What an unforgettable moment in my life! Or should I say in our lives. This is one of the most crucial and important moments of my life. At this point, the whole team was shaking hands and embracing each other, even Castro's Secret Police. The entire weight lifting team and the people in charge of making sure nothing like this ever happened defected.

The guy who threw the bag over the fence said that on his way out he picked it up by mistake, he thought it was his bag with his clothes, instead he found some money. I remember the Marines flew all of us back to Florida in an airplane. We were all laughing and yes, this story is true. Much later and only then did I get worried because Castro exploded in Cuba. He made threat after threat towards me. He claimed I was responsible for everyone's defection. Not true. I never spoke to anybody about it. You can't talk to anybody in communist Cuba about doing something like this, no way! The FBI was taking care of me. I told them about my concerns a couple of times. Back in Cuba, Castro was heard saying, "Sergio Oliva wherever you are or wherever you are hiding I'll get you."

Weightlifting

That's when I decided to leave Miami, Florida and go North. This is how and why I went to Chicago. I chose a place faraway from Cuba. I was worried that Castro would take me back by force one night in a boat.

These are my memories of my escape to freedom and I wanted to share them with you.

31

Chicago

My Kind of Town

I use to sleep with a gun under my pillow while I lived in Miami. I was worried that Fidel Castro would send a team of men and kidnap me and take me back to Cuba. I remember Castro kept saying over and over:
"Beware Sergio Oliva".
"Wherever you are, I will get you".
"Oliva you will pay." and things to that effect.
The FBI who was taking care of me asked me to pick any state I would like to go to. I recall them telling me many names of states and cities, when they said Chicago I said, "That's it! Chicago is where I want to go."
Without thinking about it twice I left the next day to the Windy City. I

was alone in a big city with no money. I did not speak the language nor did I know how cold a place it was. Certainly not the climate I was used to back in my homeland of Cuba with tropical weather.

In the beginning it was very hard for me, too many barriers to overcome. I laugh now but it was especially hard at dinner time. It was hard just to get a meal, wow! No jobs, no friends. It was like being asleep for years and then waking up and not knowing anybody, the city or my way around it.
Fortunately, I found a job in a metal foundry. It was an extremely hard job. Sometimes the temperature inside the foundry would get up to 500° Fahrenheit. Many workers had to take salt pills and many times you would be working side by side with a worker and suddenly he would not respond to your conversation. A quick glance over, and you would find him passed out on the floor. That's how hot it was.
We were making molds and sometimes the workers use to sit down and wait for the material to arrive, wasting time and money. I remember saying to myself, "Sergio, there has to be a better way." And sure enough, I found it. I built a special table to move the supplies while I was working with the first mold. The result was that I used to make two or two and a half molds everyday.

While others were making one or one and a half per day. In reality I could do it because of my physical strength and hard-working background. I was working like an animal but I was making good money at that time.

Every time I remember those days, one particular incident comes to mind. Most of the men working at the factory use to go home, eat, and go straight to bed. Not me, no! I use to go to the YMCA and do heavy weights for two to three hours everyday. One day a man from the factory approached me and said, "Bullshit, Sergio! I don't believe it." So we made a $200 bet. Without me knowing, he spied on me for days and found out it was true, so I won that bet.

Photos by Jules Freedmond   *One of Sergio's first competitions*

I worked in the foundry for five years, then one day I walked in the main office and said, "I want my check, I quit!" The people working in the main office were shocked. They called the Supervisor and he wanted to know if there was anything he could do to change my mind. Of course not, my mind was made up. I got my check and walked out.

About an hour later after I got home, someone knocked on my door. When I opened it, to my surprise, it was the President and the Foreman of the company. I invited them in. Once inside the President said,
  "Sergio if you want more money just tell us".
  "What is the problem"?
  "We will give you much more than what you are making now, we will give you better, longer or shorter hours".
  "We will even change your supervisor if you want".
  "You are such a great worker that we will do anything to have you back".
Of course my mind was made up and they could not convince me to go back.
  I said, "Thank you but that is my decision. Thank you".
After they left I could not believe they had traveled all this way and taken the time to come to my own home. But that part of my life was over and I had to move on.

Then I went to work at a butcher house, unloading, loading, and moving beef. Now, don't get me wrong, it was a very hard job as well. We had to spend hours inside a freezer with gloves, hats, heavy coats, and moving very heavy loads. But it was better than the 500°, the salt tablets, and people passing out around me all the time. I worked in this place for about 3 years.

It was not easy leaving my family behind. Unfortunately, I never got to see my father, my brothers or the rest of my family ever again. I did see my mother one time after 30 years. I invited her to the United States and finally Castro allowed her to come. When I saw her my heart and my spirit fell to the ground. I had left a powerful, pretty, young woman and now, 30 years later; I was facing, in the airport, a woman dressed very poorly, destroyed by a hard way of living. I don't have words to express what I felt at that moment. For sure it was one of the most intense, beautiful, and emotional moments of my life. To be able to embrace, hold, and kiss my mother again after 30 years, seemed like a dream. I thanked God and La Virgen de la Caridad (Conchita) for having given me this opportunity in my life again.

I took her shopping to buy her clothes. I took her to the beauty parlor to get her hair dyed and styled. And man what a difference that made! It was like night and day. She spent three months with me here in the United States and I tried to be as good to her as I humanly could. We really enjoyed this last time together and it will always be with me forever.

After all I made it ok. I met good people, made new friends, got married, had kids, and a job that I loved because I got to help people in need. I even got into bodybuilding competition and the rest, as they say, is history. I love Chicago. I feel at home here. My son and daughter were born here. So I guess I am going to die here.

Chicago has something for everybody. If you want to eat Chinese food go to Chinatown. Feel like eating Spanish food no problem; go to Spanish town. Chicago has a great diversity of people and restaurants from all over the world.

For shopping, we have the most beautiful downtown area in the United States. Have you ever walked or shop through The Magnificent Mile? It is an experience to walk through this beautiful boulevard full of trees and well-dressed people. It has many skyscrapers like the Sears Tower and The John Hancock Observatory. Its people are well mannered, not rude or rough. Also it's a laid back kind of town, it is not a rush hurry city, like New York or Miami.

What about the Navy Pier? It is a beautiful place to spend an evening with your kids and family. Relaxing, playing, walking, and enjoying a real beautiful sight.

Airports? We have it. We have the busiest airport in the United States, The O'Hare International Airport. One of the biggest in the world, if am not mistaken. You can get a plane here to fly anywhere in the world.
We also have TV shows produced here, watched nationally like the Ophra Winfrey Show. Sports? Yeah, we have the Chicago Bulls (basketball), The Chicago Cubs (baseball) and of course, The Myth, Sergio Oliva.
"I love Chicago. Chicago is my kind of town".

Trainer of Champions

They also called him "The Master", the Master of what? Joe Weider, was a businessman that I didn't trust. In my opinion, and the opinion of many, he was only after one thing — money and he didn't give a damn about whom he screwed along the way. Many times I was told by others that maybe he didn't like me because he was a racist. Personally, I don't think he's a racist. He's just a manipulative cheater that wants his way no matter what. However Betty Weider, his wife is a sweet, warm, and beautiful lady.

The problem with Joe was that when I went to the IFBB I was already Sergio Oliva, the champ. I had already won many titles and he could not say that I was one of his disciples. He couldn't say that he made me with his products, machines, or equipment and I wouldn't lie. I wouldn't endorse his products, and I'd tell it like it was. For his business that wasn't good, he wanted me to say I used Crash Weight 7, Protein 101, etc., and I wouldn't do it.

Around the same time he discovered Arnold in Europe, young, ambitious, white, unknown to the Americans and he contracted him. He brought Arnold to America and the only thing Arnold had to do was train in the morning, sleep, hang around Muscle Beach (Venice, CA), and train in the afternoon. Weider paid for his home and food and in return, Arnold would endorse everything for Joe. He even had time to go to school!

I'm not putting Arnold down, I like Arnold, but this is the truth. In the meantime, here I was, Mr. Olympia, having to work 10 to 12 hours a day and then train after work. That was hard and it wasn't right that Weider was supporting Arnold so that he could just train and face me in the Olympia.

Sometimes he would publish articles under my name and would send me a couple of $100 checks then damn when I would deposit the checks they would bounce. Can you believe it? He's a man making millions of dollars and the checks he sent me bounced? Then I would have to call his brother, Ben Weider, and he would tell me deposit it again because my brother this and that. Sometimes it would take me a month just to cash $100.

I admit that Joe Weider made bodybuilding what it is today. I realize that and admit the truth. But it's also true that he pulled all kinds of tricks, changed judges, changed votes in competitions and did as he pleased. Look what happened in the 1972 Mr. Olympia Joe changed the judges at the last minute. I was called backstage to make a line. I was first, then Arnold, and then somebody else. They kept us like that behind the curtains for a long time. Then suddenly, the judges were changed. I was asked to change places with Arnold and one of Joe Weider's associates told me. "Sergio they screwed you, they just changed the voting". Yes, they cheated, they gave it to Arnold, and people started to boo Arnold and chanted my name. Bottles were thrown, chairs broken, even Rick Wayne discussed this issue with me. Many experts and editors told me that this competition was a scam.

That was a disgrace for bodybuilding and for Joe Weider. Everybody present that night knows I won. Still today people and magazines talk about that day. I was robbed and Arnold and Joe know it.

But let's think for a moment, if Arnold worked for you, got a salary from you, represented your company and interest, and you promoted the competition were you going to give the title to an outsider? Are you going to beat your own man? The one sponsored by you and your company, the one that is costing you thousands of dollars? Come on, this is crystal clear! I had no chance but on my way out of the building, I took my shirt off and stood on top of a car for the hundreds of people waiting outside to see me. They were chanting my name and letting me know they were with me.

The story doesn't end here. In my opinion, Joe almost never printed my pictures in his magazines. And when he did, he used my worse or most awkward position pictures or when I was changing poses. He would place them next to the best photos of Arnold to proof his point. Arnold's pictures were hand-picked for the better and mine were hand-picked for the worse. Furthermore, Joe Weider had blocked me out, he pushed me to obscurity, to the corner. His magazines barely mentioned me or have my pictures printed. The majority of the big, major competitions were directly or indirectly promoted by him, or his IFBB Federation. So he pushed me out! He forced me out of the competition and without exposure of his muscle magazines I had no publicity. Joe Weider affected the success of my career tremendously not to mention all the money, exposure, and opportunities that I lost. But I wouldn't give in. I'm a rebel and the more he hurt me professionally the more I moved away and the more outspoken I became. By now most of the bodybuilders, champions, amateurs, and muscle magazine editors know, if not the whole truth, most of the truth concerning Joe Weider and I.

Most of the champions claimed they were using Joe's products when in reality all of them were using Rheo H. Blair products. This is a fact and the champs can vouch to it. Bodybuilding Pros who could receive supplies of Weider and Hoffman products were buying Blair supplements instead. Frank Zane, Dave Draper, Lou Ferrigno and Arnold Schwarzenegger all "secretly" used Blair's protein while promoting Weider's version. Among the Blair disciples were Charlton Heston, Racquel Welch, Liberace, Bruce Lee, Lawrence Welk, among others, Rheo H Blair was know as the nutritional advisor to the stars. I could write endless pages about Joe and his schemes, and his actions against me.

I'm not afraid of anybody and I'm telling you the truth, the way it is. The way it happened.

Mr. Olympia 1968

I trained extremely hard for the 1968 Mr. Olympia. I was expecting to meet really tough contenders. Chuck Sipes, Arnold Schwarzenegger, Harold Poole, Dave Draper, and many other great champions of that time. Somehow nobody showed up. I went on alone and won the Mr. Olympia Title uncontested. The only time in history that somebody wins this title without any competition. In reality, I was disappointed because I had been training and getting ready for this battle extremely well. My body was big, muscular, and cut.

I went into my posing routine and everyone was yelling, "Sergio!" "Sergio!" and they were pounding the floor. There are many stories I have heard or read about as to why these champions did not face me that day. However, I don't really know the truth. Some people say that when they found out I was competing they all quit. I don't know what really happened, but I will list some of the contenders' excuses that I have read about or heard.

Harold Poole

Got a promotion to a big New York business and affected his training due to work and time.

Chuck Sipes

Won the Mr. World competition and performed strong stunts that day and was tired. He did not feel he should go against me that day. According to witnesses, Joe Weider advised him not to face me that day.

Dave Drapper

Movies and guest appearances affected his training and decided not to show.

Arnold Schwarzenegger

He announced to the IFBB that he would be competing in the Mr. Olympia. Somehow or something changed his mind and entered the Mr. Universe in London, England instead. Coincidentally, it was the same day as the Mr. Olympia.

At that time I was working 10 to 12 hours in the metal foundry and training three hours every night after work. It was extremely hard and people were amazed and could not believe that I did it. Anyhow, I was there in shape, muscular, and ready to battle but nobody showed up that day. Excuses or not, I guess I will never know. But I know that I won Mr. Olympia in 1968 uncontested.

Mr. Olympia 1969

To provoke mind-blowing thoughts, I would walk around backstage wearing a long butcher's coat. Finally I heard my name called it was my turn to pose. I waited about four more minutes before I came out. As I walked out to the stage and went by Arnold, I took my coat off and said to him "Take a look at this", and flared my lats. Like letting him know it was over and in reality it was.

He was destroyed. His jaw dropped in shock and he looked at Franco Columbo for support. By that time, my fans were yelling "Sergio, Sergio, Sergio!" I came out and blew a kiss to my fans. Then I raised my arms and the house went down. I smiled and really was enjoying the moment. I went from pose to pose slowly. I was in control. The fans were trying to get close to the stage in an attempt to get a closer look at me. The chanting of my name made all my hard work meaningful. Then I left the stage.

Arnold and I were called back to the stage. Back on the stage, neither of us would flex a muscle. Some people yelled, "Pose, pose!" finally Arnold hit a pose. I raised my arms over my head "Sergio, Sergio, Sergio!" the fans shouted. Arnold hit another pose; I hit the most muscular pose I was in total control and at ease. As I switched poses I kept telling Arnold "Hey baby, look at this one" in reality he didn't have a chance as he said in his two books.

The chanting of my name left no doubt who was Mr. Olympia, I smiled I won that day, and retained the Mr. Olympia title. Then suddenly Arnold moved closer to me and kissed me in the head.

To be honest I felt that the entire audience was on my side; I felt the warmth of everybody present. I remember many people wore t-shirts that said Sergio is King. Camera lights were flashing everywhere. The audience was chanting my name I enjoyed every minute. I was Mr. Olympia once again for the third time in a row. It was my moment of glory and I was sure to savor every minute, every second of it. This memory would last me a lifetime. All my hard work and training paid off, I had won. I raised my arms in victory and I was proud, proud to have won and proud to have pleased my fans.

Consequently, Arnold talked about this event on p. 97 in his book titled "Arnold Education of a Bodybuilder" and I quote "I saw Sergio Oliva in the dressing room in the Mr. Olympia 1969 for the first time. It was jarring, as if I had walked into a wall. He destroyed me, he was so huge, and he was fantastic. There was no way I could even think of beating him. I admitted my defeat and felt some of my pump got away. But I had been so taken back of my first sight of Sergio Oliva that I think I settled for second place before we walked out on stage. Sergio beat me only 4 to 3 and that was a surprise I thought he should have beat me 7 – 0. I never like to admit defeat but I thought Sergio was better there was no way about it".

However, if you look at Arnold's eyes in the picture that was taken when Joe Weider was handing me the trophy for the 1969 Mr. Olympia title his expression was that of a man who was promised something and expected to win but let down. Arnold's eyes were an open book.

And here is something to think about, in his book, "The education of a Bodybuilder", on page 94, Arnold said Joe Weider use to pay for his apartment, and gave him a weekly salary so he could have time to train 5 hours a day. In exchange he would supply Weider with photos and product endorsements to advertise in his magazines. Talk about the difference between day and night, I had to work 10 to 12 hours a day at the metal foundry and then after a hard day of work I trained for 3 hours. I had to work all day to make a living. If I had the same opportunities Joe gave Arnold, I can't even dream how far I would have gone.

Arnold, Jack and me at the Mr. Olympia 1969

Mr. Olympia 1970

Photos courtesy of Jack Merjimekian

Mr. Olympia 1970

When they called my name the crowd went mad, screaming my name. Arnold signaled me like saying after you, Arnold looked good, big, and strong. But I had separation, top definition, and mass. I gave them a powerful front lat spread, Arnold answered me with one of his poses, and we battled each other hitting different poses. Finally I kneeled with my arms above my head, and I knew Arnold couldn't beat me then. I was tremendously humongous, shredded, and muscular. All this time the fans were rooting for me "Sergio, Sergio" others were yelling "Arnold", "Arnold". We turned around so judges and fans could check our muscular wide v-shapes. I knew I had the best tapered of both. The crowd growled.

Police were keeping the fans from reaching the posing platform. The fans were screaming really loud by now. Some of my fans were holding up pictures of me and yelling, "Sergio is King". The Mr. Olympia 1970 came down to a fierce battle between Arnold and me.

However, Arnold tricked me in New York in 1970, when we were competing against each other on stage. He told me "I've had enough. What about you?" I said "Me too." then he said, "Let's get out of here" and he did a gesture with his hand like saying let's go. I walked in front of him but he did not follow me, instead he stayed behind. He had tricked me and had made a hand gesture to the audience insinuating that I had quit. What a dirty trick! Fortunately, I noticed he wasn't behind me and I was able to react I said, "Oh shit!" and returned to Arnold's side and then the fierce pose down started all over again.

I raised my arms into a front double biceps. Shouts, screams, feet pounding were heard all over the auditorium. Then I did the twisting one arm bicep pose. Arnold was doing his own routine, and people yelled "Sergio, Sergio". I raised my arms isolating the muscular muscles in my back. My fans loved it and I remember smiling at them. When the announcer gave Arnold the title, the crowd became infuriated they were yelling, booing, throwing pop bottles, anything they could get. I believe the score from Weider's judges was 3 to 4 in favor of Arnold. So Joe Weider got his man Arnold, a white man, for his magazine covers. Don't' forget that 1970 was still a very discriminatory time in the USA? A Spanish, black man may have not been what Weider magazines needed to sell to the public.

As Arnold said in his book, "Encyclopedia of Modern Bodybuilding" and I quote "certainly his blond, Nordic, looks made him an ideal candidate for representing bodybuilding for the public." He was talking about Andreas Cahling.

What does he mean by this? Does he mean that a white blond champion was better to do bodybuilding ads and better for magazine covers than champions with dark skins? At that time, sure it was. Like the book by

MuscleMag International Muscle Quest by Gerald Thorne and Phil Embleton said on p. 88 "Sergio's name remains relatively unknown among the public and one simple and ugly explanation might explain this, racism. At the time he became involved in bodybuilding segregation was still legal in the USA the Civic Rights Movement was still fighting its greatest battle. The majority of consumers were white, and they bought supplements and magazines that featured white bodybuilders. If Sergio had been white, we might remember Arnold as an obscure Austrian bodybuilder that competed against Sergio."

Joe Weider needed a white Mr. Olympia. Ok, now you can use your intelligence, did Arnold really beat me? Or did the role of politics and special interest groups like Weider's organization, which Arnold was under contract with did?

I'm a sportsman, sometimes you win and sometimes you lose. I know how to accept defeat when I have actually been defeated. But Arnold never beat me. Not once, not in 1970, not in 1972. Yes, I was beaten by the judges and the Joe Weider IFBB organization. Not by Arnold.

I don't believe in using any of these garbage tactics. When I compete, I compete with the best men that are present. I'm a champion, you either win or lose. Champions don't need tricks, I like to win or lose fair and square. A real champion doesn't' need gimmicks. Interesting enough, if you look in Joe Weider's 2006 book, on page 175-179, Joe talks about this incident, but you make your own conclusions.

Photos courtesy of Jack Merjimekian

Mr. Universe 1971

Everyone knows I beat those guys in London in 1971. Bill Pearl refused to stand next to me while on stage. Why? I was given 2nd place; again I was cheated one more time.

When I read in magazines that I was beaten by Bill Pearl they some how don't mention that most experts agreed that I was the real winner, that night. I have accepted defeat others time, when it's true, and only when it's true, but not because of Joe Weider, or because I'm black, Latin or not a kiss ass and in those years it was hard if you were not a white bodybuilder. But again, politics was involved, friendships, etc.

In the next few pages I've included an article that Arthur Jones, the inventor of Nautilus Exercise machines, author of hundreds of muscle articles and a legend sent to different muscle magazines at the time but never got printed. Why? I've included it here now, courtesy of Arthur Jones. Read it yourself and make your own conclusions. I'm sure that by now you know that I was not only facing the top champions of that time but also the unreal and unfair politics that was taking place then.

Deland Beach, FL

Photos By Inge Cook-Jones

The Incredible Myth

Deland Beach, Fl, photo by Inge Cook-Jones

Oliva shows his remarkable shape and bulk. He is equaled by no one else in the world

Deland Beach Fl, 1972
Photos by Inge Cook-Jones
Courtesy of Arthur Jones

Physique Contest
Article by:
Arthur Jones

Having attended some, not a lot but some, physique contests, and having observed the overall scene in weight training circles for more that 50 years, it was obvious to me that the declared winner of such contests is not always the right choice. All too frequently, the winner is determined for political reasons.

During the period from the 1940's until 1970 several black men entered the Mr. America contest who should have won but did not win because they were black. Then in 1970 the "powers that be" decided it was time for a black winner and so they looked around very carefully and selected one, Chris Dickerson, and he won the title that year. But he should not have won, Casey Viator created a sensation with the audience, and should have won but instead took third place. Comparing Dickerson's physique to that of Casey's was a joke, but the decision was based on politics.

For 25 years we had discrimination, then it switched to reverse discrimination, having been impossible for a black to win it then became "politically correct for a black to win".

For a period of many years Bob Hoffman, owner of the York Barbell Company, controlled the Mr. America contest with an iron hand. He decided who should win and it was a requirement that a potential winner spend several weeks training in York, Pennsylvania immediately before the contest so the winner would appear to be a York trained man.

Later Joe Weider did much the same thing when he started promoting contests. The result being, in both cases that the right man did not always win. Which is why I have always had a rather low opinion of such contests. I have never been an admirer of Joe Weider myself. In a race, or in almost any athletic competition, the winner is usually obvious. An exception being fights that are won on the basis of a decision rather than a knockout.

Several years ago I watched one of Larry Holmes' fights on television, a fight that he won on a decision, but in my opinion, I believe the other guy actually won the fight. Then, a few months later, Holmes came to visit me and tried to get me to give him a lot of money for the supposed "privilege" of training him for his next fight, this supposedly being an opportunity for me to get a lot of favorable publicity for my business. But I told him thanks, but no thanks. In the first place, I have never paid anybody for an endorsement, and in second place it was a "no win" situation for me, if he won following my having training him I would get little or nothing in the way of credit, but if he lost it would be blamed on me. Apart from ethical considerations, turning him down was a wise move on my part because he lost his next fight.

In my opinion, paying celebrities for "endorsements" is outright fraud, the people who are chosen to endorse my products have done so because they like them, not because they were paid.

And the people who have any of my equipment pay me for it, at full price, yet I still get about a dozen requests a month from people wanting to get some of my equipment free in return for their endorsement. Such people are wasting their time, it will never happen.

But the action that I recent most was the outright screwing that they gave Sergio Oliva in the Mr. Universe contest London in 1971. For several months immediately prior to the contest a series of articles called "The Bill Pearl Story" was published both in this country and in England, and if you were dumb enough to believe those articles you would believe that Bill Pearl, if not God himself, was certainly a God of some kind.

I trained Sergio Oliva for that contest and went to London with him, so I clearly really saw just what happened. During the pre-judging Pearl was asked to step up next to Sergio, but he looked down at the floor, waved his arms in a gesture of defeat and moved backwards away from Sergio, ultimately refused to permit a side by side comparison.

Compared to Sergio he looked utterly ridiculous, and he knew it. Yet he "won" the contest, or, in fact, he "fixed" it.

For a period of several years prior to that contest, a very wealthy friend of mine who had a beautiful home just outside London had been paying all of the expenses involved in promoting and conducting that annual contest, while permitting the promoter to keep all of the income as clear profit, he did so because of his interest in weight training but did not want to connect his name with the contest. So the promoter had a very good thing going for himself.

I was staying in my friend's home and very shortly after we returned there following the contest the phone rang, it was the contest promoter calling to apologize for what had occurred. When my friend realized who was calling, he told him… "Wait a minute, Oscar, I can't talk here, let me go to another phone". Then he motioned for me to pick up the phone while he went to an extension, so I heard what was said. Oscar said… "I am sorry about what happened today. He sent an article to several magazines in which he assured the readers that the contest had not been fixed, the tone of the article clearly indicating that he was rushing into print with a denial in anticipation of an accusing article from me.

And I wrote such an article, a satire which I called "The Pill Bearl Story", and in which I called the contest the "GRABBA" in "BLUNDON" and called Sergio "Hergio Saliva", it was, I thought, really quite funny. But Peary Rader's wife Mable refused to print it in Ironman. So we then had a situation where Oscar was offering denials in an attempt to answer accusations that were never made.

During early years, thousands of pictures were taken at that contest every year, and hundreds of these pictures would be published in various magazines during the following year. Following that contest there were only a very few pictures published, and only a few showing Sergio, because they could not find any other picture that would fail to show just what occurred.

And a number of totally untrue statements were published, they said that Sergio was "fat", when in fact he was as lean as a well-conditioned race horse, and I have pictures taken immediately before the contest to prove it. They also said that you could see him "shrinking" during the contest, losing his "pump". But in fact he was never pumped, posed cold. They provided Bill Pearl the equipment and space required to pump prior to the pre-judging and the contest, but refused to provide anything for Sergio.

These lies were repeated so often that even Sergio started to believe that he had been fat, realized the truth only when I later showed him the pictures we took immediately before the contest.

Nearly a year earlier, Arnold and his friend Franco Columbu visited me in Florida, and while they were there Arnold met a man that we called "Turkey" so the following year, while I was training Sergio in Florida, Arnold used this man as a "spy" in an attempt to learn just how well Sergio was doing. He planned to enter the London contest, but did not want to lose to Sergio.

Being clearly aware of just what was going on, this being obvious from the questions that Turkey asked Sergio, we decided to try to blow Arnold's mind. So we started feeding Arnold lies through his spy, at first Sergio's arms were 22 inches then 23 inches then 24 inches and so on, while his body weight rapidly increased to nearly 300 pounds. We figured that Arnold would either get fat trying to get bigger than Sergio, or get too small in an attempt to be more muscular than Sergio, in that in either case he would lose. But we apparently over did it, scared him off, because he did not show up for the contest.

Turkey continuously asked Sergio how much I was paying him, and Sergio told me about this question. I paid him nothing apart from buying him a coach-class airline ticket to London.....

Fairly recently Arnold told Joe Cirulli that he had never met me. Sure. Well, as it happens, I have hundreds of pictures of Arnold that we took in my house, in my gym, and elsewhere.

I first saw Arnold in Central Africa in 1968, when he put on a posing exhibit sponsored by Reg Park, he was, I believe, 20 years old at the time. I met him again in California in 1970, and then he visited me in Florida in November of that same year. And I saw him at a contest in Columbus, Ohio, and talked to him for several hours afterwards.
So he might not know me, but I certainly know him.

In my opinion, Arnold, in his prime had one of the two best physiques in history; it would be difficult for me to decide just which was best, Arnold's physique or that of Sergio. If both were at their peak, I would not object if one was declared the winner, their physiques were different, but each was in a class far above any other.

Deland Fl Photos by Inge Cook-Jones

Sergio Oliva a true legend in the sport of bodybuilding

The Herculean Physique of Oliva
Photos Courtesy of NABBA

Sergio with Park, Pearl, and Zane at the Mr. Universe 1971   *Sergio at 250 pounds*

Mr. Universe 1971

Photos Courtesy of NABBA

Hitting a front lat spread, displaying muscles of massive lats, chest, and shoulders.

Mr. Olympia 1971

I have good memories of my travels abroad. When we traveled through England for the Mr. Universe (1971) and then I flew to Paris for the Mr. Olympia (1971). I did enjoy it. I met and made good friends like Fox, and Serge Nubret, people whom I admire and enjoyed their friendship, very professional and fun to be with. Wherever I went people recognized me and if they did not know me they wanted to know who I was. People asked me for my autograph and wanted to have a picture taken with me. The women were real pretty but most importantly, they were friendly, some were crazy, yes, some were hyper, but in the long run I met friends and enjoy it. Europe was beautiful. I really loved traveling to Europe.

After my competition in England for the 1971 Mr. Universe I flew to Paris to compete for the Mr. Olympia but Joe Weider had other plans, when I got there I was told I could not compete. I was banned for having competed in another association. According to Joe I had broken an IFBB rule. What kind of shit was this? I had never heard of this rule, nobody had ever told me! I concluded among others that this rule was made especially for me. What a commotion it was, people were complaining, fans were upset, you have to realize that I was Mr. Olympia for 3 years the only man to really challenge Arnold. I was the man to beat. In reality without me, the Olympia that year would have been a joke, a fake. People were yelling, and complaining, because they had come to see Arnold and I battle and it wasn't going to happen.

Finally after many struggles and discussions, I was allowed to be a guest poser. I was ripped, huge! And Arnold was given the green light for the Mr. Olympia title that was another trick Joe Weider and his organization pulled on me. I should have been allowed to face Arnold that day. I was ready but Joe had already decided that Arnold would be Mr. Olympia for 1971 especially, with me out of the way. Anyway when I took the posing platform people were yelling my name and they were pounding the floor. What a scene, I was massive, humongous, cut and symmetrical. I was ready for this competition. That was the first time I had heard about Joe Weider banning someone for competing in a competition outside the IFBB. And it worked so well for him too. If I'm not mistaken, this rule is still in effect. I wonder why Joe didn't mention the 1971 Mr. Olympia in his book.

In other words, if you wanted to compete, make money, get exposure, you had to go through Joe. Joe Weider would own you and if he didn't, then you would be pushed aside and banned from his powerful magazines and competitions. You would be forced into the dark. You would be destroyed economically. This was the truth about making it into bodybuilding. Why can't bodybuilding champs be allowed to compete or get exposure anywhere they choose? Why couldn't they speak their mind about Joe Weider or the IFBB? After all, we lived in a free country.

New and young bodybuilders keep this in mind. You must try to change the system or you too, no matter how big, strong, or cut you are. No matter how much fans admire you, or how hard you work out you will be manipulated and have to do as you are told.   In my case I refused to be owned or manipulated. I paid a big price for that so athletes beware.

Everybody present that night knew and still knows I was the better man.

Sergio's genetics comes only once in a generation

Chicago 1971

Photos courtesy of Jack Merjimekian

Mr. Olympia 1972
Essen, Germany

Backstage was full of tension, deep breathing and wandering eyes were scattered about the room. The contestants were tensed. Champions were pumping and oiling their bodies. I felt many eyes staring at me. The fans were making noises in the auditorium. The atmosphere was drenched with electricity and magic. The moment of truth had finally arrived, months of hard blowing, gigantic workouts, diet, and pose practicing would soon be seen. I took my warm-up clothes off and everyone stared at me. Yes, everyone's jaws actually dropped wide open in disbelief. I was massive and shredded, I could tell

Courtesy: of Denie

that many champions, felt they had lost right there and then. Just like it happened to Arnold in the Mr. Olympia 1969 Championship contest, he said it in his book, The Making of a Bodybuilding pp. 97, "Only his sight beat me".

I am ready! Ready to storm the stage! I trained really hard for this competition. I watched my diet and I trained harder than ever. But once in a while I ate whatever I wanted. Coke, rice, beef, I will always remember one particular day, after a workout, I stood in front of the mirror and for the first time I got scared. I was humongous and symmetrical, so big that I thought my body was going to explode. I was so damn shocked with my own physique that I had to sit down for a while, about 5 minutes or so and I worried that I was so damn big!

You have to realize that I wanted to beat not only Arnold, in Germany, but also Joe Weider's underground manipulation. I had to be at my best and I was! I was at my peak, huge and ripped! I also thought that if they cheated, and I would lose, the public would always know the truth. My name was called; I took a deep breath and walked out slowly to the platform. I smiled, nodded my head and hit my first pose. The audience went wild! The feeling of euphoria ran all over my body, I loved competing, I loved bodybuilding and I loved the fans.

I walked onto that stage and raised my arms. Silence filled the room. People were shocked! Then the audience exploded with applauses. I smiled, nodded my head, and began posing. What a feeling! The audience and I became one. As I moved from pose to pose people yelled, clapped, whistled, stood up, and started yelling "Sergio!" "Sergio!" each and every time I tensed my muscles into a new pose. I moved around to the next pose, inhaled some air, and slowly hit the next pose. The crowd went wild! I smiled, bent over, and flexed my muscles harder. The house went down! There was nothing that could stand in my way. I felt at the top of the world. This is what I had been training for and waiting for, the moment of truth. "Come on give it to them Sergio!" yelled the audience.

Courtesy: of Denie

I could see some faces and hear their voices. The fans were excited! Some were out of their seats. Man this is what competing is all about! I felt the adrenaline running through my veins. I was enjoying every minute. I liked the contact with my fans. I felt the universe had come to a stop, but it was really only a couple of minutes long.

When I finished, I raised my arms into the victory pose. That really drove everyone crazy. I looked at Joe Weider and his face was pale white. I could see it in his eyes. An expression of disbelief, mixed with defeat. He knew there and then, that I had won. And if he cheated me like he did before, people would surely know and disagree and talk about it for years to come. I walked off the posing platform with the same feeling that a gladiator must have felt as he walked out of a fight in the coliseum.

I crossed paths with Arnold. Arnold was big and cut but in reality he did not match my calves, thighs, v-shape, forearms and of course, my waist. We looked at each other for a couple of seconds. Just like boxers do before the first bell. But deep inside his eyes I could see that he also was impressed. Deep inside he knew that I, Sergio Oliva, The Myth, was the champion that night. No matter what Joe Weider and his organization might pull.

Then we battled each other, Arnold hit a pose and I bettered it. Fans yelled "Sergio!" "Sergio!" "Sergio!" He did a double bicep and I did a front lat spread. The crowd roared with excitement!

I then hit the most muscular pose and he did the same. I squatted down to a double bicep; people chanted my name, "Sergio!" "Sergio!" This was war! There were other great champions competing that night like Columbo, Zane, and Nubret but all eyes were on Arnold and me. In fact, the competition was so intense that night that it felt like nobody else was there. Arnold was no match for me. I was humongous, symmetrical, and ripped. There's no way Arnold could have beaten me that night, unless of course, they cheated.

Boy what a night that was for me! A night of contrast! Feeling and knowing that I was in the best shape of my life! The warmth of the audience welcoming me and yelling for me! The sweats, the emotions, the lights, are all wonderful things that I just can't find words to express my feelings.

On the other hand, to have the Mr. Olympia title taken away from me gave me a feeling of emptiness, which varied from rage to sadness. To be cheated like that in front of hundreds, to see that something that I earned was taken away from me, the only way they knew how changing the judges and the score card at the last moment.

Everybody present knew I was cheated. Fans, reporters, even some editors of muscle building magazines, said I was cheated. So did others in similar lines of business. It became a very controversial topic. Interesting enough, this most important competition between Arnold and me was only briefly mentioned in Joe's new book.

Behind the stage the competitors shook hands; the big night had ended. After everything was said and done, they can't hide the fact that I, Sergio Oliva, a Cuban man, was one of the greatest champions of this sport.

If somebody would ask me Sergio are you the best? I would answer with

a reply that Bruce Lee, the great, late, Chinese Kung-Fu master champion once said: "If I tell you yes, you are going to say how conceited I am and if I tell you no you are going to say what a liar".

Everybody that I talked to, competitors, editors, reporters, and fans told me there was no way in hell that I could have lost, unless the most outrageous, cheap, manipulation of the judges was involved. Unfortunately, the latter happened.

If I am not mistaken, even Arnold has admitted that he did not win in 1972, that it was only politics. It's my understanding that after the contest Joe Weider put the promoter of Europe out of business because he refused to have competitions with the winners predetermined by Joe.

Wayne Gallash

Life guarantees a chance
not a fair shake
___Anon

London, two days after
The Mr. Olympia 1972

Wanstead Flats, London two days after the Mr. Olympia 1972   *Photos: by Wayne Gallasch*

Unknown photographer

Mr. International 1973

Let me tell you what happened in the Mr. Azteca International in 1973, I remember Eddy Sylvestre (a Mexican bodybuilder champion and contest promoter) was running the show, I came on the stage and I dared Arnold that was sitting in the public to face me right there and then. Without Joe Weider's judges protection he did not face me. Why not? If you are the best why not prove it? What are you afraid off? Columbu went up and battled me that was no match. Arnold later said he couldn't do it because he was under contract. Bull! Your reputation is on the line; the eyes of the world were there. In my opinion, he was scared that without Joe's protection and in a real competition he could have lost. So he found a way out, an excuse.

In December 1940, Mr. America, John Grimek was traveling through the United States doing posing exhibitions and weight lifting. One man by the name of Karl Morberg stood up and challenged John and John full of confidence accepted. At the end Grimek triumphed as the true champion he was. He was not afraid, not intimidated. In my opinion, he could have accepted my challenge and proved in front of the audience who was really the champ or better man. He opts for saying "His contract won't allow it", etc. I bet you anything that Muhammad Ali or Bruce Lee wouldn't have given it a second thought and would have stepped forward to prove they were the best. The real champ, screw the contract, the media, and the commotions, to prove he was the best. I wouldn't have given it a second thought, when you are the best there is nothing to be afraid off. Are you number 1 or not? The same thing happened when Arnold and I were invited to be guests on the Tomorrow Show with Tom Snyder. Arnold and I had a heated, huge discussion. When all of a sudden a curtain was raised and there it was an Olympian bar with 300 pounds. Snyder said, "Ok let's find out who is the strongest, the best man for once and for all".

I walked over and picked the weights 3 times over my head. Just like that. Then I told Arnold it's your turn Arnold responded by saying he wouldn't do it. "I did not come here to lift". Snyder said, "Well Arnold, Sergio picked it up 3 times why cant' you do it?" Then Arnold again used the excuse of being under contract. And he walked out of the stage pissed off and left. Once again he had the opportunity to prove that he was better, but did not stand for the challenge.

An excuse is a lie guarded

_Jonathan Swift

On Arnold

Don't you think for a moment that I don't like Arnold. That is not the case. I respect Arnold as a man and as a champion bodybuilder. When Arnold came to America some people did use him, but he was smart and lucky and got what he wanted. He also married Maria Shriver Kennedy, a very successful and intellectual woman that is part of one of the most prestigious families in the United States.

Arnold "The Austrian Oak"

Photo Courtesy: David Landau

He turned things around and became what he is today. When I talk about him, I talk about the athlete the contender, the opponent, and the adversary. It is like Sugar Ray Leonard and Tommy Hearns or Joe Frazier and Muhammad Ali. I am sure they don't dislike each other, but in the ring they were there to destroy each other.

Just like Arnold and I, the confrontations we had were unmatchable in the sport of bodybuilding, as were those of Frazier and Ali in boxing. He was the toughest man I had ever competed against, and I got into the best shape of my life to compete against him. He also had a remarkable physique to stand next to me and compete against me. When Arnold was in Chicago we had many good workouts and he even came over for dinner many times, despite the fact that he was training to compete against me.

I believe Arnold brought the sport of bodybuilding to the public eye with his movies in an astounding way. You cannot talk about Sergio without talking about Arnold, or about Arnold without mentioning me. I don't think there will ever be such rivalry and fierce competition in the sport of bodybuilding like we had.

The Myth and the Austrian Oak working out in Duncan Gym YMCA 1969 Chicago.

One of the greatest of all times

Check Oliva's v-shape! - 1977 Paris   *Photo Denie*

Mr. OLYMPIA

1984/85

Mr. Olympia 1984 with Samir Barnnout
photos courtesy of Robert Kennedy

Twelve years after my last competition, I went back to compete for the Mr. Olympia Title. I received a phone call and was promised that this time; the judges were going to be fair. Joe Weider took this moment of opportunity and made the competition a night of speculation. My comeback drew tremendous publicity. However, in the end, he used me one more time!

My former wife, Arlene, convinced me to use the diet Frank Zane used for his last Mr. Olympia contest, but it did not work for me. I was in tremendous shape but maybe a little bit off my best. Everyone that was there that night or has seen the video agrees that I should have finished in the last five, not in eighth place.

I was big, cut, symmetrical, and maybe a little shaking posing, but still, if you look good at the pictures and tapes, you can tell that my body was more aesthetic looking and my waist smaller than most of the competitors that finished within the last five.

When I was called to eighth place the audience began to boo, and yell in disappointment. They knew I was cheated again. You could clearly see this and hear it through the audience's response. Even the TV sports commentator remarked that "eighth place for Sergio was not a favorite one. They are all very unhappy with this call".

I walked slowly to the stage raised my arms and the audience went crazy, I walked to the edge of the posing platform and my baby boy, Sergio, just a few months old, was handed

to me. I presented him to the audience and the audience went crazy. The TV sport commentator said, "Sergio has stolen the show".

I walked back to the podium, and while holding my son in one arm, I said "Congratulations to the best man" "No matter first place, third place,

eighth place, or seventeenth place, no matter, I will always be The Myth forever!
And I walked away. The house went down and the people went crazy chanting
"Sergio!" "Sergio!" "Sergio!"

Photos courtesy of Denie

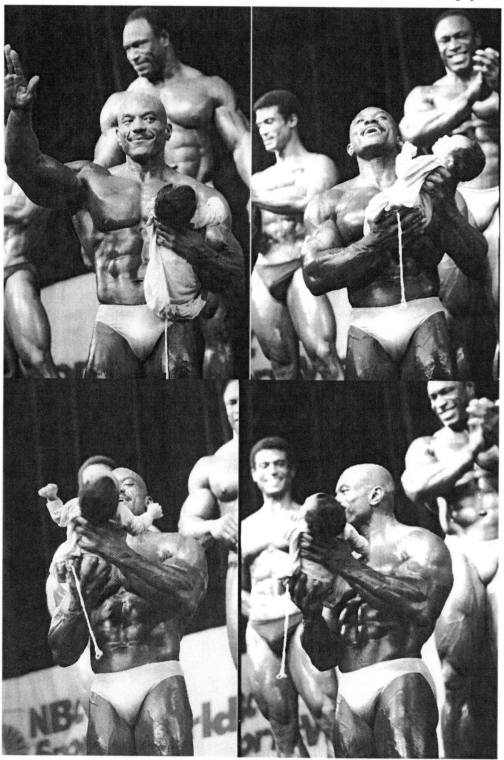

Sergio presents his new born son to the audience as Lee Haney and Mohamed Makkaway look on

Sergio's placing - not a favorite with the crowd

Mr. Olympia 1984

Later I found out through somebody important in the Joe Weider organization, that no matter what condition I would have been that night, even if I would have been King Kong, Joe Weider had already given me eighth place long before the competition had even began.   My place with fate had already been decided. The 1985 Mr. Olympia same scenario, same results, same placing, by now it's was more than clear that the IFBB will never change as long as Joe Weider was in charge. So I said good-bye.

This was my last Mr. Olympia contest.

With Lee Haney, Chris Dickerson and Bob Paris

Mr. Olympia 1984
Photos - courtesy of Robert Kennedy Musclemag International.

Weider picked the winners, when he thought it was time. Nobody won if he didn't want them to. Remember in bodybuilding, he made the deals, sold the supplements, and equipment, etc.

With Tom Platz and others great champions

64

So if you didn't accepted his ways or were a part of his schemes and manipulations, you were out of luck. That is why many top contenders left the competition arena and retired, they didn't want to put up with the grueling workouts, diets, sacrifices, and then be pushed to third or fourth place because they were not under Weider's contract. Don't forget it is called Joe Weider's Mr. Olympia contest.

Joe Weider controlled most of the competitions, most of the magazines, so if he signals you out, you were relatively out. You would get no exposure and no articles would be printed about you. You would be left out of the game, while in the meantime; he was bringing in new people to the spotlight. Weider had the power to destroy your career or make it.

This is why until a way is found to make competition fairer and more accountable, more and more top athletes are going to get out of the game. Of course, the money, the big prize, and the dream to be a champion is what keeps most of them competing. But there has to be a better way and a fairer way to compete. Not just a one-man organization making all the decisions.

When people ask me how do I feel about Joe Weider having cheated me of so many triumphs, good moments, and money? My answer is always the same, "The people know the truth. I can't change the world, but there are pictures, tapes, and eyewitnesses. If you are not blind you will see the truth behind it all. I leave everything to God".

Photos courtesy of Robert Kennedy

Sergio always thrilled the audience with his incredible muscles

Sergio's last competition Mr. Olympia 1985

65

Chapter 2

History's Greats

Do you remember the man that won the title, "The World's Most Perfect Developed Man" Do you remember his ads in comics books? Did he inspire you as a young boy or as a young man?

Thousands of young men bought his courses.

I think this was the first time the general public got to meet a muscle man.

Then Steve Reeves hit the public. He became famous with his Hercules movies in the 1950's. He was very handsome and he had a very symmetrical body with a nice v-shape upper body. I believe these two champions, were responsible if not for all for part of what bodybuilding is today.

Steve Reeves photos courtesy of George Helmer and Steve Reeves Intl. Inc.

Photo by Russ Wagner
One of the most proportionate men in the history of bodybuilding

Young people everywhere wanted to improve their physiques. Sure there were other champions but these two champions will always have to be mentioned when you talk about bodybuilding's greats.

I met Steve Reeves when I was traveling in Europe conducting seminars. He was a very likeable person, easy to talk to, and an easy person to get along with. I remember one time I was posing on the stage and I looked at him and his eyes were wide open in shock. We had long talks. This great champion was always a very down to earth person. It was a privilege to have known him.

Another great in my eyes was John Grimek, he was fantastic, he had a very impressive body and was also very strong. He had a good sense of humor and was a great dancer. He used to dance a lot, just like me. Steve had the looks; women would go crazy around him and John had a Herculean kind of strong body. I was fortunate enough to have met him too. These were the only two bodybuilders I looked up to.

Steve Reeves Photo courtesy of George Helmer and Steve Reeves International, Inc. Steve Reeves 1950 Mr. America photo by Tony Lanza www.Steve Reeves.com

Even though there were other greats before them. Champions like:

- Eugen Sandow alias The Great Sandow
- George Hackenschmidt alias The Russian Lion
- Arthur Saxon
- Herman Gomer
- Sigmund Klein
- Louis Cyr

Arthur Saxon (Arthur Henning) was a strongman performing in Europe in the 1980's. Arthur Saxon died in August 6, 1921 at 43 years of age.
Eugen Sandow was the most famous bodybuilder in the early days in the sport and the first modern bodybuilder. Born Friederich Wilheln Muller in April 2, 1867 in Prussia (now part of Germany) and died in 1925. In 1902 at the age of 35 his measurements were, 5' 9¼", weighed 202 lbs, neck 18", chest 48", biceps 18½", forearms 16 ½", waist 30", thighs 26"and calves 18 ".

John Grimek

| *Eugen Sandow* | *Arthur Saxon* | *Sig Klein* |

Photo courtesy of www.sandowmuseum.com   Photo courtesy of R. Christian Anderson, Ph.D

Sig Klein was born in Germany in 1902, he moved to Cleveland, Ohio in 1903. As a young boy he became fascinated with strongmen shows and by 17 years old he was lifting weights. Klein tested equipments, movements, and exercises for the fastest and best results for building muscle size, definition and good health and longevity. He died at age 85 in 1987. He helped develop the standard techniques of today's bodybuilding.

This chapter wouldn't have been complete without mentioning these old timers that contributed to the history of bodybuilding. In fact, Eugen Sandow was promoted as "The Worlds Strongest Man", in the United States. It has been said that he was responsible for the boost of barbell sales.

Vince Gironda, "The Guru", his theories and ideas were ahead of his time. His training philosophies in the gym were extremely controversial. He helped trained many actors and champions.

Then we have some of the baby boomer bodybuilding champions like:
- Dave Draper alias The Blond Bomber
- Rick Wayne (also a great writer)
- Frank Zane
- Lou Ferrigno
- Danny Padilla -The Giant Killer
- Robby Robinson-The Black Prince
- Casey Viator
- Serge Nubret
- Mike Mentzer alias Mr. Heavy duty
-

Dave Draper reminded us all of the blond beach boys of California, portrayed in Frankie Avalon and Annette Funicello's, beach movies during the 60's. At 6'1, with 230 pounds of muscle a great champion, a heck of a guy.

Dave Draper photo courtesy of www.Davedraper.com

Lou Ferrigno was the famous Incredible Hulk from the hit show during the 70's. His measurements were 6'5, 270 pounds. Big Louie, a fantastic champion.

Mike Mentzer, a true pioneer, with his Heavy Duty system. Arthur Jones' Principle influenced him. Mike improved on Arthur Jones principle and took it over and beyond. An incredible outspoken and extremely intelligent fellow. A great champion.

Arthur Jones invented the Nautilus machine, and his Principle of Intensity. An outstanding very bright man, some people referred to him as a genius. , And he is. I also met him when I went to train with him in Florida. I respect and admire the man.

And last but not least we have the millennium generation
- Flex Wheeler
- Shown Ray
- Gustavo Badell
- Ronnie Coleman
- Jay Cutler

And many more ....

Bodybuilding history is still being written right now, tomorrow, the day after and I'm very pleased to have been part of this history.

Flex Wheeler 2000 Arnold Classic 1st
Courtesy of www.teamflex.com

Danny Padilla- The Giant Killer
www.originalgiantkiller.com
Mr. Universe- Mr. America –Mr.USA

Ed Corney - Mr. Universe with Nikko
www.edcorney.com

Robby Robinson" The Black prince"
Mr. America –Mr. Universe- Mr. World
www. Robby Robinson.net

Photographers

What is a photographer? He is an artist. An artist captures subjects and moments in time. Pictures bring us memories and make us relive the past. What would the world be like without pictures?

Champion photos have traveled around the world. Photos have made bodybuilders eternal. Thanks to great photographers such as: Denie, Art Zeller, Jimmy Carusso, Russ Warner, Wayne Gallasch, John Balik, Robert Kennedy, Mike Nevex, Chris Lund and many others.

Wayne Gallasch photographing Sergio in London two days after The Mr. Olympia 1972

These muscle photographers have made it possible for young men around the world to get to know the muscle champions in the four corners of the world. Thanks to these photos, young men around the world have been inspired and started bodybuilding in order to improve their physique.

That is how it happened to me when I was a child in my native Cuba. I use to see the famous muscle men in the front covers of magazines. Little did I know then I was going to be on the covers myself.

Were you inspired by the pictures of the muscle man in the comic books, or the pictures of Steve Reeves, Grimek, or me?
These photographers made the champions appear bigger than life, especially when certain poses became the bodybuilder's trademark. Such as Steve Reeves, John Grimek, and the Victory Pose for me.

The photographers create legends through the lenses of their cameras. They captured the best and exposed the top champions' image to thousandths making them known and idealized.

What would a muscle mag be without great pictures? Bodybuilding photographers are a special kind of people. And they deserve a special mention in my book. We owe them a lot.

Training

As I drive through Chicago on my way to the gym sometimes people say hello to me when I stop at a red light and I wave to them. By the time I get to the gym, my mind is already set up in anticipation of what is to come. My body is anxious and hungry for that gut feeling you get from hitting the weights hard.

I open the gym door and a warm feeling goes through my body. As I walk, people greet me and say hello on my way to the second floor where I train at World Gym. Sometimes I see a couple of beautiful women getting ready for a tough competition and I flirt with them. We laugh some, and there are times when they ask me a couple of questions and I answer the best that I can.

When I workout I don't like to talk I keep to myself. But prior to working out, I usually say hello to everybody in the gym. I stop sometimes to tell somebody "come on, one more rep or you can do it" or some words to that effect. But once I start my workout routine I don't talk and I don't like to be interrupted. I move without interruptions from one exercise to the next. I describe my own workouts as crazy and brutal.

A proportionally balanced huge Sergio

Now I'm in front of my passion, my mind turns off all other distractions. I begin my warm-up and now I'm totally involved. My concentration is so strong that I actually feel every muscle of my body connected to my mind. I feel like I can talk to them "grow, grow, separate". As my hand grips tighter onto the bar, my body explodes into my workout. For the next two hours it's as if I don't hear or see anything. The only thing I can feel is my blood rushing through my muscles. Sweat pours out of my head, arms, and all over my body. My workout is nonstop, only stopping between sets to breathe deeply for about 30-40 seconds; maybe a minute. My concentration is so deep that even if the gym collapsed, or noises were heard, it wouldn't affect me. These two hours are dedicated to my body, mind, muscles, and the weights. I'll go through reps, sets, and exercises like it's my last day at the gym. I don't care about tomorrow

or next week, it's all about here and now. I feel incredible as my workout reaches the end. It's like I did not want it to end. It's like the feeling you feel when you are out with a beautiful woman and you don't want the date to end but it does end.

My training is kind of crazy. I like to use the pyramid system. I'll use a certain weight to warm-up and then I'll go on adding increments of 25 pounds sometimes passing 325 pounds or more. Depending how I feel that particular day. I really never change the exercises; I do the same ones year after year. Why change? It works for me.

Between sets maybe I'll walk around for a minute to recuperate then I'll hit another set. Once in a while I'll walk to the water fountain and take a zip of cold water. That's it. Then I'm back again hitting the weights. As I said before, I don't like to talk when I'm training nor do I like to waste time when I'm at the gym. I'm there to train and train hard not waste time.

To be honest I sometimes train by feeling (as I feel) but this doesn't mean I don't have a routine or a specific way, or order to train, I do. But many times I change, add, or delete an exercise for that particular day. Many times when I'm finished and I'm walking to the shower I change my mind and go back out, and maybe do 50 dips or go to the preacher curl or Scott curl machine and hit my biceps. I'll do this after a grueling, heavy workout that lasted maybe 2½ hours. That is why most people can't keep up with me in the gym. I don't do this to impress anybody, or compete. This is just the way I am.

Photo by Denie

Photo by Denie

One time Joe Weider sent Franco Columbu and Arnold to train with me, to spy on me, to find out what I was doing. Both of them had a hard time keeping up with me, but Franco Columbu came close. Franco is a very strong champion but Arnold could not keep up and left.

I always try to protect my back, low back, elbows, and shoulders. I know if a bodybuilder hurts his back, elbows, or shoulders, his career could be finished.

I never did exercises to make my rib cage big; I always paid attention to balance and symmetry. If I worked my shoulders, I worked my front, sides, and rear delts paying attention not to over develop my trapecious muscles. Each muscle that I work, I work all the muscle sides, and if I work on my thighs, I train the front, outside, and inner side of the thighs. I do it this way to train my whole body.

Many times I see a great champion with a 57-inch chest or bigger, but his thighs or calves do not match his upper body or he has a roid belly that sticks out like a sore thumb.

You have to keep a balance between your neck, waist, and calves. How many times have I faced an opponent as big as me? The difference was my waist, thighs, and calves. That is the trick. Balance is the word.

You want to be huge? Fine, but you must keep balance. Champions that quickly come to mind are John Grimek, Steve Reeves, Bob Paris, and Shawn Ray they all have balance, and aesthetic looking bodies that remind us of a great sculpture. Not grotesque, out of balance, nor an out of proportion body. Keep focus, and always concentrate on balance, proportion, and symmetry.

When I do bench presses to warm-up I place 185 pounds on the bar. I never really lock my arms to protect my elbows and not to release the stress in the muscles. I hit about 50 reps, from here sometimes I'll go to the bars to do dips using no weight I'll do 20 super fast dips. Going low but never locking the arms at each rep. I like to vary the reps and weights I use from day to day. Depends how I feel that particular day.

When I use the lat machine, I lower the bar moderately, slowly, spreading my lats with each rep as much as I can. By now I feel pump, my veins are almost exploding, from here I might go to the incline bench and then to shoulders, sitting down in front of the bar using a very wide grip. I press the bar up never locking at the top placing the stress on the muscle at all times. On days when I work my legs, my workouts are not quite as long as the other days.

One evening at the gym, I was asked by Frank Marchante, who had traveled from Miami to Chicago to take pictures of me for my book, how much longer was I planning on working out? My answer was "as long as I live or my health allows me too". I love to train. I love to feel in contact with every muscle of my body. Now I train 2 hours a day, 6 days a week but in my competition days I would train 3 to 4 hours a day.

I could never be in a diet for a long time, I love to eat, and I'm a meat lover. So the longest I've ever been in a diet is 3 or 4 weeks at the most. And this includes when I would wake up in the middle of the night hungry and I would say "the hell with it". Open the refrigerator door and eat anything I wanted to. But tomorrow I would be in a diet again.

I cannot eat fish or tuna for more than a few days. Then I have to have a steak. I never drink alcohol maybe once in a while at a party or on a special occasion. That goes for coffee too. I love to party, and dance, oh yeah, I like to party! In the past, I would work 12 hours a day, train 3-4 hours, and then go dancing all night. Bodybuilding champions use to ask me all the time "how do you do it"? I don't know how, I just did it! I only know that if I ate well and got 2-3 hours of sleep that was all I needed. I can't even imagine how my life would be without working out, the gym, the smell, and the noise of the iron being moved up and down.

Incredible Mass

Photo by Denie

Only when I'm finished and have taken a shower do I talk to some people, especially to young and new bodybuilders. I always make the time to talk to youngsters, they remind me of me. What about if those muscle guys at the beach back in my native Cuba had no time to talk to me when I was young? I probably wouldn't be here writing this book now. I have always answer questions, take pictures or sign autographs with newcomers if they ask me to. Know why, because one day these people could be great champions.

Many people have asked me about Sergio Jr. They want to know if he lifts weights. Is he planning on following my footsteps? My answer has always been this "I would like for my son and daughter to have the best education possible. I don't want them to go through what I went through. Sergio Jr. has already entered some competitions. However, it's too early to know if he is going to go all the way at this point but whatever they decide to do, they will always have my support and my help of course. I will always be there for them".

As I sit back listening to some music and enjoying the drive back home through Chicago streets, I feel all my muscles alive. If I was tired from work, now it's all gone; I'm a new man. I love working out, I really do.

Courtesy Jay Cutler Mr. Olympia
www.jaycutler.com

Courtesy: www.shawnray.com

Photo courtesy :www.Labrada.com
Lee Labrada –Class with Mass

Photo courtesy of Frank Zane www.Frankzane.com
Frank Zane three- times Mr. Olympia

The Cop

I'm going to tell you about one hell of a scare I had as a police officer. I received an emergency police call and when I got to the site, I found out that a good friend of mine was barricaded holding his two kids at gunpoint. Can you believe it? I went up to try to talk to him. We talked for almost four hours; the moment was very crucial, full of tension and anxiety as I tried to bring some sense back to him, running against time until he dropped the gun. I had to take him in, it was a very emotional moment as you could imagine. I have a bunch of intense moments to tell but this one in particular comes to mind because I knew him and his family personally. It was one of the most terrifying, toughest, and unforgettable moments I ever had as a policeman.

Another one that comes to mind is a day that I pulled over a speeding car. When I got to the driver he showed me his Doctor's ID and told me that he was a surgeon. He was in a hurry to reach the operation room because he had to do an emergency surgery. I said, "Follow me", and jumped into my police car, turned on the siren and lights, and escorted him all the way to the hospital. We made it there in just a few minutes.

Years later when I was shot twice in the abdomen with a 38 special, I drove myself to the hospital and after they stabilized me, because of my body mass and muscle, and my condition of blood loss they were worried about operating me. They were afraid. They had a doctor's meeting with all of the surgeons and the head surgeon. When they told the head surgeon "We have a humongous black police officer full of muscles between life and death, the head surgeon said "Nobody touches that man but me" he took his tie and coat off. "I'll operate this man right now myself". Well he did and saved my life.

When I woke up the next morning the doctor came to see me, and said, "Do you remember me?", and I said "Holy cow, what a damn coincidence!" he was the same man I escorted with my patrol car years ago. Then he placed his hand on my shoulder and said "You helped me save a live, now I have saved yours, we are even." and he walked away. Talk about life's coincidence, fate, or God's hand.

After a couple of days in the hospital, and not being able to see my son, who was only two at that time I got a little anxious. I got out of bed with pajamas and everything and walked out of the hospital. I walked about five blocks to go see him.

Incidentally, that day my Captain went to see me and when he could not find me, the whole hospital was looking all over for me. The doctor and the captain got in the police car and went looking for me all over town. When they found me I was very weak, and refused to get into the car. I insisted that I had to see my son; finally they agreed and promised to take me there if I got in the car. I saw my son for about 40 minutes and then went back to the hospital.

I loved being a policeman. I got the chance to help people in need. I felt something very special when I helped the elderly and especially children. This is my way of giving something back to a community that has given me so much.

I'm Chicago and the Chicago Streets are me. If you are ever in Chicago keep your eyes open I could be driving next to you.

Wanstead Flats, London two days after the Mr. Olympia 1972 Photo: by Wayne Gallasch

Emergency

I had been arguing with my former wife, when suddenly, she called me a "son of a bitch". I got so mad that I just slapped her. It was bad enough that I hadn't seen my mother for over 30 years and so I didn't need someone putting her down. She then turned around and went to another room and the next thing I knew; she was pointing my 38 revolver at me. I never thought she was going to pull the trigger so I ran towards her to take the revolver away. We were struggling and in the process of taking the revolver away, I moved the barrel against me, she pulled the trigger and shot me in the stomach. If it weren't for the shape I was in, I wouldn't be writing this book today. She shot me only inches away from my stomach.

I took the revolver away from her and pushed her out of the way. I asked her to take care of Sergio Jr. who was 2 years old at the time. I told her "I'm going outside". I hadn't realized yet that I was shot. When I turned around I felt a sharp pain in my stomach. I looked down and saw a blood spot. I looked to the floor but saw no blood. Suddenly I realized I was shot and that I had internal bleeding which is much worse. I know that God, and La Virgen de la Caridad (Cuba's most worshiped Virgin) were with me that day. I owe my life to them.

I walked to the elevator, which at the time, I was living in a new condominium building on the third floor and "shit" the elevator was not working! I took the stairs. I couldn't wait. I ran downstairs to the garage, got in my car, and drove to St. Francis hospital, bleeding. I only made it to the parking lot. Fortunately many people knew me there because since I was a police officer I had taken many injured people there before. When I stepped out of the car, someone asked me, "Champion what do you got?" I answered, "What I got is a bullet in my stomach!" and I fell on top of a chair. Everybody started running around to get help and I was taken to the operating room.

After the operation when they were taking me to my room, I heard a Greek friend of mine that I love with my life saying "Cumba, Cumba, you are here, you made it". Three weeks later I was walking around in the hospital and ready to go home. Once again, I would like to thank God and La Caridad for watching over me that day.

Mike and Ray Mentzer

The phone rings and I pick it up, on the other side of the line I hear the familiar voice of Frank Marchante calling me from Miami. He gave me the news about the passing of the Mentzer brothers, two days apart from each other. Mike passed away on June 10, 2001, he was 49. Ray passed away on June 12, 2001, he was 47.

I was shocked. I felt a chill running up and down my spine. How could it be? They both were young. I knew they both had health problems but this? A deep feeling of sadness went through my body. Once we traveled to Europe together to do many posing exhibitions/ competitions. They were younger than most of us and we called them "the boys" affectionately.

The sport lost one of its superstars. Both of them will pass on to bodybuilding history, especially Mike with his concepts of the Heavy Duty System. I personally will never forget Mike.

Mike and Ray Mentzer, you will always be remembered.

Training Concepts

Bodybuilding is a way to develop muscle mass, shape, and symmetry using progressive weights. As you get stronger, you add more weight and your muscles grow in size and shape. Developing your own body requires knowledge about exercises, diets, nutrition, concentration, and balance.

Repetition or Reps

Repetition or reps is when you go through one repetition of an exercise.

Sets

A set is when you do an exercise for various reps. Example, 1 set / 10 reps = 1 exercise repeated 10 times.

Correct Weight

I always selected heavy weights for a least 6 to 8 reps and then continue forcing reps to 12. Don't use too heavy of a weight or too light. If you can do more than 10 or 12 reps it is too light. You should get to the last two reps with effort; keep adding resistance to continue growth. This is the concept of weight resistance. So remember to make progress, add weight. When the rep becomes easy to do, it is time to add weight and the cycle repeats itself over and over again.

As you grow stronger, and progress in strength and size, your training should become more and more intense. Then as you continue to progress, you could adopt a split routine. That is when you workout some body parts one day and the other body parts the next day.

Concentrate on the basic exercises, working on the major muscles of your body. At this point, forget the smaller muscles; later you will have time to work all of them.

You should perform your exercises with full range of motion and don't try to hurry and use a medium speed. The basic exercises are:

- Squats
- Dead lift
- Curls
- Bench press
- Barbell press

- 1 or 2 abdominal exercises like crunches or reverse crunches

Warm-up / Cool Down

Don't turn your warm-up into your workout. What I personally use is the Pyramid Principle, for example, I'll go 155 pounds for x amount of reps and I'll go up in weight every set. Then I'll go down, that is my warm-up and exercise set.

Free Weights vs. Machines

My personal opinion and like many others champions is that there is nothing like barbells and dumbbells. I believe free weights are better, more demanding to the muscles, than machine or cables. I would say they have built mostly every top champion in the world. One of the advantages of free weights is price. Don't get me wrong now; there are some machine exercises that are as good as or better than free weights. Of course, machines are safer; I also use machines in my workout. If you can, use both. Both have their good points. Remember to always, but always, warm-up and cool down. Never sit down after working out, walk slowly, move your arms, and neck to cool down.

Muscle Bound

Not so long ago people would say you were muscle bound (lack of flexibility) if you developed your body using weights. Not true. Nowadays, football players, baseball players, boxers, and other athletes use weight resistance to get in shape. I think that old tale is over with.

Personal Log

I know people like Frank Zane, Mike Mentzer, and others use to write down everything that had to do with their training. They used it as a feedback so they didn't have to memorize everything. Keeping a diary will help you keep track of your exercises, weights, reps, progress, and the foods you eat. It's also a good idea to take pictures to monitor progress.

Back Support

Use a belt when you are doing heavy weights. I use one in the gym most of the time.

Wraps

Most people use wraps especially if they have weak or injured joints. They use it on their knees and elbows when they're doing heavy exercises. I have used them on occasions.

Headband

Use one to prevent perspiration from getting into your eyes. Many times I have used one.

Gloves

Many of today's bodybuilders use gloves. Gloves will help you with the grip. This is all right, but I personally don't use them.

The Gym

Find one that is close to your home. Many people don't feel like driving especially too long, after a hard day's work. Make sure there is adequate equipment including machines and free weights, plenty of space and it's well ventilated. Check the shower, make sure it's clean .It should also not be over crowded. Parking lot is something to keep in mind.

Home Gym

You can develop a great body working out at home. Some champions like Lou Ferrigno use to train at home. Space should be one of the first requirements, you also need a bench that changes position, a barbell and two dumbbells at least, and if possible an exercise machine, an exercise bike or a treadmill will be great. Make sure there is good ventilation, better fresh air, and wear warm clothing if it's cold.

Clothes

Personally, I like to wear a t-shirt or a tank top. Loose fitting clothes are a good idea. This is your choice of course. Wear something warm to keep the body's heat, like a warm suit, sweatpants and a sweatshirt.

Rubberized Suits

I see a lot of people using it. They can endanger their life. They don't do anything for you. So please be careful. Sweating burns calories yes, but it's a dangerous way to do it, don't use it.

Best Time to Train

Choose a time that you can work out with no interruptions. This is your time. Let no obstacle stop you from training on the days you have chosen. Give your training time your undivided attention.

Over Training

If you feel tire the next day, can't sleep well, or are not making the progress you expect, then maybe you are over training. Watch out!

The Pump

When you train you fill a muscle with blood. At the end, your muscle remains filled with blood, and appears larger for a while. Some champions believe that when you achieve the pump, it's time to call it quits. Not me. People have described this feeling with all kinds of different expressions and remarks. This is the famous pump and you can get addicted to it.

Muscle Pain

This is common the day after a nice heavy workout. If this is your first time working out be careful. Many people are so sore the next day they can't even get out of bed to go to work or even walk. So please start slowly. If it hurts STOP! Find another exercise that works for you.

Size

To develop size, you must use the basic exercises that at the same time build strength and power, like bench presses, squats, chins, bent over rowing, seated press, curls, and dead lift. Heavy weight combine with extra calories and proteins will make you gain size. You want to be big? **Eat like a big man**.

Definition

To achieve definition you have to combine nutrition, weights, cardiovascular stimulation, raising your heartbeat, and breathing. Of course, using more calories for fuel will also let you lose fat. You can do it by restricting your carbohydrate intake but many others swear by calories. Many people think that achieving maximum definition is a mystery. If you decide to remove carbohydrates make sure to eat some, so you have energy to train and do your cardiovascular. You must reduce your body fat to 7% at least so veins and muscles will show.

Cardiovascular Exercise

Cardiovascular exercises is steady and non-stop, it should last at least 15 minutes and maintain the heart at 70 or 80% of your maximum heart rate. There is no doubt that cardiovascular exercises are extremely important for a strong heart. When you do it, your heart beats faster and you breathe deeply more oxygen.

This extra stress makes the heart pump blood through your blood vessels, like any other muscle, it must be used. How do you know you're you've done enough? By monitoring your own pulse for 6 seconds and then adding a zero. For example, 13 beats plus zero equals 130 beats.

Personally I don't need to check my pulse; I know when I'm having a vigorous workout. The symptoms are clear, my heart beats faster, my breathing is deeper, and I'm sweating more.

Properly done cardio will not only burn calorie and fat while working but for hours after finishing working. Muscle burns more energy than fat. Walking is a safe and simple cardiovascular exercise for all ages. Bicycling is also real good. The use of a treadmill inside the gym to walk or run is much safer and it doesn't matter how the weather is outside, try it. Some others are, rowing, playing tennis, basketball, etc.

Stress Signs

Diarrhea, constipation, palpitations, anxiety, sleeplessness, skin problems, hair loss, and many other conditions could be stress related symptoms.

Nutrition

Nutrition plays a big role in bodybuilding. Eat healthy. Check the chapter on nutrition.

Relaxation

To me exercising is a kind of relaxation, but you must learn to relax. Listen to your favorite music, take a walk after dinner, and stop thinking stressful things for a while.

When you are stressed out, the first thing that happens to your body is something that you don't need. Adrenaline production shoots out causing the fat cells, from all over, to move into your blood so it can be used as energy. At the same time, your body is producing another hormone called "Cortisol". Somehow it gets stored in the belly as fat.

Mental Attitude

Concentrate on going for your dreams. First you must really want something, and then go after it. You have to have a dream to reach your goal. A positive attitude is of real importance to lose body fat or to gain muscle weight, to get muscular, to make it or quit, don't be a quitter. Focus on what's going right and things that can be changed. Otherwise don't think about it, forget it.

Humor

Humor is extremely good for better health. Most women love a man with a good sense of humor. Men that smile a lot, have better personalities, better health, less anxiety, less tension and better looking women. Humor is a health tool, use it, and laugh. Believe it or not, laughing helps circulation, does wonders for digestion, is excellent for lowering blood pressure, and keeps you optimistic and raises your self-confidence. You will not find a better medicine or drug than laughing. In my personal case many people ask me how I do it. How do I keep in shape after all these years? Well I believe that one of the tools that have helped me is my way of being, happy, easy going, laughable, and friendly.

Genetics

Genetics is heredity pass down from generation to generation, like blue eyes. Keep in mind that genetics will limit your own body development, no doubt about it!

Concentration

Concentrate when you are working out, concentrate on your muscles, and imagine your muscles growing with every set. I'm a believer that your mind can help your muscles grow though concentration. Do it!

Deep Breathing

Have you ever watched a baby breathe? In and out, deep and even, slowly and easy, they are using their diaphragm. So start to breathe deep, slowly though your nostrils. To exhale simply reverse the process slowly. Don't strain! Never, I repeat, never hold your breath when you are doing heavy training. Ever! Try to exhale when you are moving the weight into the hardest part.

Sleep

It is recommended to sleep at least 7 to 8 hours a day of uninterrupted sleep for maximum growth and reparation. Of course this is up to you, everybody is different.

Aging

You are as old as you feel, that is the truth. There is no reason not to develop a nice body if you are older. However, you are going to develop muscles more slowly; you will gain fat in the wrong places. If you are 40 or 50, you won't win a Mr. Olympia title, but I'm sure with the proper training you could develop a body that will be the envy of men half your age. As for myself, I still train everyday.

Working Out Partner

A training partner must use the same routine no matter the weight used. Having a partner is great because there are days when you don't feel like working out and your partner motivates you and pushes you. At then end of the day, you had a good workout. I use one 99% of the time.

Safety

Safety is very important in all the exercises you do, especially the squat and bench press. It is dangerous to work by yourself. I've gotten into some problems before. One day I was working out to my maximum alone in the bench press and I got stuck. The bar was in my chest and nobody to help me. I had to roll the bar of me and it was really scary. Be careful!

Caution

Always protect your elbows, shoulders, lower back, knees, and heels. If you injure any of these parts your training will be held back or you will have to stop training for good. If at any time during your workout it hurts, STOP! Find a different exercise to work out that muscle. By all means, work around it. Again, be careful with these body parts.

GIMMINICKS

There are always new gadgets in the market, some have merits but most of them are a fast way to make a buck. I repeat myself there are no substitutes for barbell, dumbbells or machines. Be alert.

Photographer unknown

Training Systems

These systems have been around for years. Some people have classified them to make it easier; I will list the most popular ones:

Pyramid

Ascending sets or pyramid up, this is the one I like to use, for example, I warm-up with 180 pounds and then keep adding weights to the bar until I reach my limit. Then go back reducing the weights. Mix with super-sets.

Peripheral Heart Action (PHA)

Consist of 4 or 5 exercises in sequences. The idea here is to improve your cardiovascular system to raise your fat reduction, and raise your heart rate to your target rate. PHA improves your strength, gives you size, and helps your cardiovascular capacity.

Force Reps

Do a set to failure, and then your training partner will help you with the last two reps, because otherwise you will not be able to complete it.

Supersets System

Training opposite muscles, for example biceps against triceps or bench press against row. I have used it all my life as a bodybuilder for over 40 years in combination with pyramid up.

Negatives

When you can't lift the weight anymore then your training partner helps you lift the weight and you lower it.

Descending Sets

Start by doing a set with x amount of weight and the next set by using a lighter weight, and keep lowering the weight as you keep doing the same sets and reps.

Split Training

There are different ways to split a routine, for example, triceps, chest, and shoulders one day and biceps, legs, and mid-section on another day. Different kinds of split training can be design, depending on your time, energy, and goals.

Bi-Set

Combination of two exercises done right after the other, for same body part.

Cheating

Getting the weight up with a swing then finishing the movement with more of a strict manner.

Tri-set/Giant Sets

Train the same body part for three sets then hit another muscle for three sets.

Priority Training

Training first your weaker spot or muscle. If your thighs are weak begin training hitting them first.

Rest –Pause

 You perform one single rep close to your max, pause, and then do another, pause, and so on.

Training to Failure

Failing to do the last rep in a set, you should use a weight that when you get to do the last rep you will fail.

Muscle Confusion

Doing a variation of the same exercise to confuse the muscle, for example, barbell curl, and lat pulley curl.

Circuit Training

You must complete an exercise circuit in a target time limit. The idea here is to help alter your metabolic rate to control your body fat. It is done in a non-stop fashion, rest, and it's repeated again two or three times.

Intensity

There are many ways to achieve intensity, heavier weights, shortening the time to do a set, more reps, more sets, longer time, etc.

Achieving the Pump

The muscle feels like it's engorged by blood.

Straight set

The basic system, the one used by beginners and intermediate bodybuilders. Very effective training system. Perform 3/6 sets of an exercise.

Pre-Exhaust

You pre-exhaust a muscle close to failure, and then move to a compound exercise immediately.

Partial Rep

Doing partial reps when you are to tired to do full reps.

The Rack

Using the dumbbells down the rack, put one down, pick the next lighter one.

One and a Halve

Do a complete rep, follow by one half rep, alternating one full one half rep.

Slow Training

The slow concept requires a positive contraction of ten seconds and a negative contraction of four seconds. Many people say it's effective because it eliminates momentum. In my opinion it's boring.

DENIE

Posing

What is posing? Posing is showing your best and hiding your weak or worse part from the judges and audience. This is what posing really is. Posing is hard. It takes hard work to be a good poser.

Appearance – Hair should be short. Long hair for sure will distract from your shoulders. The color of your **posing trunk** should match your skin color. I think a solid color will makes you look better. Massive bodies will look much better using high cut trunks.

Oil - Don't forget oil. Oil will give highlights to your muscles, many champions use baby oil, so you can too. Bodybuilders shave their body hair to look better and make their muscles stand out more. You can use a lotion, razor, or electrical shaver, depending on your personal preference.

Tan – Don't neglect a nice tan, your body should be tanned or you can apply what many bodybuilders use now, one of those instant tans. Make sure you apply it evenly and according to instructions, so you don't end up with a line here or there. If you are black you should tan your body anyways so it won't look washed out. A tan will do wonders for your physique in the posing platform, No matter your color. Keep in mind that a deep dark natural tan will help you look more define, probably you are because of the water loss.

Confidence – You should look relaxed; try to give a positive and winning attitude. Move, walk, and act with confidence. You're the winner! Practice, practice, practice! Move slowly with grace from one position to the next. At the same time, put all your strength and will into the poses. Tense your muscles forcibly. Don't look dead. Smile. Show them you are in control! Don't be a victim of mind games, don't let anybody influence you. Backstage warm-up, pump up, don't look around you, what for? You're the winner, people will be looking at you, "wondering", concentrate on you and your body, not in what or who is around you.

Three times Mr. Olympia

Oliva's physical perfection combined with rugged muscularity. Awewsome!

Photo Courtesy of Robert Kennedy-Musclemag International

Peak – The only way to learn to peak for a competition is through experience and timing. Every one of us is different, and you have to practice dieting and training to achieve your peak or to be at your best for a particular competition.

Many times champions are a little bit off peak by one day or two before or after a competition. This of course is not an easy task and the only way to get it right is to practice and try it. Have someone take pictures of you as you go through your training. Then every week compare them with each other.

In my case, I just stuck to the essentials when I walked into a contest I was ready to undress, oil and go. You should plan how you are going to spend the day of the competition. What are you going to eat and do? Some champions lie in the sun to get rid of excess water. Others will walk around to unstress and others will watch a movie or read a book. Take time alone to get focused, hanging -out with others can be distracting. As I said before, we are all different and this is something that you and only you can decide.

Pumping – This is also something that you have to learn to do by trial and error. Some people like to pump the day before but most of us do some kind of pumping before going out on stage. Some do weights, some do cables/springs, and others do stretching. When you come out, smile. Keep your head up, you are in command, you are unique, act and feel confident. You will pass this feeling onto the judges and the audience, no doubt about it. This is the moment you've been waiting for. Try to enjoy it.

Many champions have lost a major contest because they never learned how to show off their bodies correctly. Many champions have become famous using a particular pose that allows them to show their best body part to the audience. When you practice, remember there are some basic kinds of posing required that may vary between organizations. Here are some of them:

- Front Lat Spread
- Front Double Biceps
- Rear Lat Spread
- Side Chest
- Relaxed Pose
- And of course, the Pose Down where all bodybuilders, try to out pose each other on the stage. You must, I repeat, appear confident! Radiate energy and believe in yourself. Posing will refine your muscles, add definition, and give you that finished look.

Mr. Olympia has gone through some changes and new developments will continue taking place in the near future.

What a physique!

Photo Courtesy of Robert Kennedy-Musclemag International

Music – Let's talk about the music. Choose music that goes with your personality, and better yet, with your posing routine. You want excitement and attention! Don't use a boring low tone music that is not going to give you an edge. You want to pick up people's spirits. You want people in the audience to get excited, to lift their emotions, and to have fun. The music also has to be the right length, long enough to allow you to do your routine. Once you've decide on the music, practice posing over and over again.

Photographs –Take your pictures from a low angle to appear taller. Backgrounds should not distract from you, white or black backgrounds look great so do simple colors. Keep in mind the sun for shadows.

Posing is an art. When you are ready to walk off the stage, do your best, most impressive pose and walk away. I never practiced posing in the gym in front of the mirror I always did all my posing at home. I never bothered with a dramatic presentation like many do. I just went out, did eleven or twelve of my best poses for couple of minutes and left. But that's me personally. However in this chapter I'm giving you tools that may work for you.

Puerto Rico 1972

Photos Jack Merjimekian

Sergio Oliva displayed such muscularity even off stage

Puerto Rico 1972

Admiring fans in Sunny Puerto Rico

Photos Jack Merjimekian

Beautiful Lisa Brewer / www.Lisabrewer.com

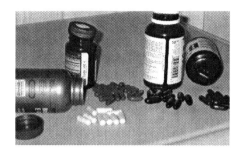

Vitamins

There are two kinds of vitamins, water- soluble and fat-soluble. Water-soluble are flushed out in the urine. The other kind of vitamin, fat-soluble, is stored in the body. There are 23 classified vitamins; they are organic and found in living things. Each of them performs different functions in the human body. Make sure you eat or take them. The human body needs vitamins.

Carbohydrates

Carbohydrates develop glycogen. Glycogen is fuel or energy used by the body to move muscles into action. It's the main source of fuel for your muscles. It's excellent for the recuperation process. After working out, your body is in need of it. It's a big part of the American diet. Very important to bodybuilders' training.

Protein

The most important source to a bodybuilder, the building block of life, to add weight, muscle, and bulk; very essential to grow. The word protein is derived from the Greek. I really don't believe too much in using extra protein powder. I have used it sparingly but never for too long. Extra protein is a waste of money and it might be hard for your kidneys. There are two kinds, vegetable and animal.

The late Mike Mentzer agreed with me on this one. The amount of protein a man or a bodybuilder requires depends on his size, work, and kind of training he does.

Fats

Reserve energy supply for the body .Fat is high in calorie, some come from animal sources. This is bad fat. Fatty acids are insoluble in water. Fats carry the fat-soluble vitamin. Olive oil, corn oil, etc. are much better.

Minerals

Minerals are a combination of protein, fats, and carbohydrates. They are essential in a person's diet, especially to a bodybuilder. Vitamins won't function without minerals. Minerals work together with hormones, enzymes, amino acids and vitamins. The body must use minerals to maintain itself. So it is important to make sure you get minerals in your diet. Talk to your doctor for more info about any dietary supplement.

Vitamins

Vitamin A-Beta Carotene
A fat-soluble vitamin. Good for vision, skin and mucous membranes.

B-Complex
Good for the immune system, nervous system, heart, also an anti-stress and mood enhancer.

B-I-Thiamine
Aid normal digestion and formation of blood.

B-2-Riboflavin
Carries energy required for life of cells.

B-3 Niacin
Also required for energy, good to reduce bad cholesterol(LDL) and raise good cholesterol (HDL).

B-5 Pantothenic Acid
Need it to produce energy, fights microbes and stress, it's also known as the anti-stress-vitamin.

B-6 Pyridoxine
Necessary for metabolism of amino acids. Fights fatigue, anemia, kidney stone, and some neurological symptoms.

Folic Acids
Help with production of red blood to carry oxygen to all the cells, important to maintain nucleic acids.

B-12 -Cyanocobalamin
For formation of red blood, for normal growth, nervous system Excellent.

B-15-Pangamic Acid
Works as an antioxidant-helps recover from fatigue.

Choline
Help normal flora in your intestines - needed for the thinking process.

Inositol
Good for hair, neurological disease, lower cholesterol level, protect heart.

Biotin
Construct protein, white cells, fights germs and helps immune systems.

Paba
Formation of blood cells, good for sunscreen, reversing gray hair.

Vitamin C-Ascorbic Acid

Slows arteriosclerosis, blood clots, shortens duration of colds, in others words, it boosts immunity.

Vitamin D-Calciferol

Strong bones, teeth and heart.

Vitamin E-Tocopherol

Reduces risk of heart disease, cancer, Alzheimer's, a very good antioxidant, slows the aging process and helps with degenerative diseases, against infections. Excellent.

Vitamin K

Aids in blood clotting, important in liver function.

Vitamin P-Bioflavonoids-Rutin

Good for hypertension, infections, colds, and gums infections

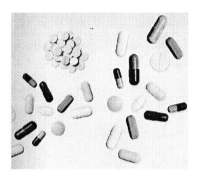

Minerals

Boron

Helps with bone loss in women.

Chromium

Will cut cholesterol, give you energy, help you gain muscle and lose fat.

Calcium

Helps bones and teeth, aid blood to clot. Regulates heart, good for vitality and energy.

Cobalt

Needed to produce red blood cells to stimulate growth.

Cooper

Helps formation of red cells.

Flourine

Protects your teeth.

Iodine

Needed for healthy hair, nails and teeth, necessary for thyroid gland, growth, and energy.

Iron

Helps to make hemoglobin, carries oxygen into the blood, can be toxic.

Magnesium

Regulates the heartbeats, helps regulate high blood pressure.

Manganese

Maintains sex hormone, nerves, and brain.

Potassium

Balances water in the body, helps high blood pressure, energy levels.

Selenium

Helps the immune system, body growth and aging. Men need a good supply of selenium.

Sodium

Balances water in the muscle and body. It's known as salt.

Sulfer

Helps the liver, gives you shining hair, it's also important for nice looking skin.

Vanadium

Helps muscle grow and develop, also helps teeth and bones.

Zinc

Helps tissue functions, impotence, resist diseases, aids fertility. Zinc is necessary for function of prostate gland.

Fiber

There are two kinds of fiber, soluble and insoluble. Soluble is found in fruits, insoluble is found in wheat, grains and cereal. Both are low in fat. They help you with regularity, not a nutrient, and it is good for cholesterol and high blood pressure.Will lower your risk to colon cancer.

Enzymes

A complex protein necessary for digestion process, some of the best are Bromelain and papain.

Sun

Needed by the human body, you need to be exposed 15-30 min a day to activate enzymes, stimulate hormone production, and improve nutrient absorption. But sun is also the responsible for wrinkling, skin will become old looking. Keep it in mind and stay in the shade for looking young.

Amino Acids

They are components of protein. Some are produced by the body others must be taken from food. They must be taken between meals not with protein. There are 22 Amino Acids .

Alanine

Good for the immune system, regulates metabolism.

Arginine

Tones muscle tissues, helps the sperm content in males, helps physical and mental alertness.

Aspartic Acid

Good for immune system, stamina, and endurance.

Carnitine

Used for intense workouts, reduces angina attacks, and helps liver and kidney disorders.

Cysteine /Cystine

Anti-aging, detoxify the body, antioxidants.

GAMMA -BUTYRIC ACID (GABA)

Helps nerves impulses to the brain. It could release GH.

Glutamic Acid and Glutamine

Helps brain functions, mood elevator and brain stimulant.

Glutathione

Respiratory, anti-tumor agent.

GLYCINE

Stimulant for the brain, aids in swollen prostate, produces glycogen.

Histidine

Helps arthritis, dilates blood vessels.

Ornithine

Muscle building substance.

PROLINE

Helps increase thinking ability. Good for wound healing.

SERINE

Produces cellular energy, helps with pain.

Taurine

Helps heart and central nervous system.

Tyrosine

Regulates emotional behavior.

Valine Need it for positive hydrogen balance in the body.

THE LIPOTROPICS

They prevent accumulation of fat in the liver. There are four, Methionine, choline, inositol and betaine. They also increase resistance to disease.

ENCYMES

Complex proteins necessary for digestion of food. They release vitamins, minerals and amino acids and keep us healthy. Lacking one could make a difference in your health.

Digestive Aids

Poor digestion means poor absorption. Digestion begins in the mouth, thoroughly chew all your food. Digestive enzymes are found in fresh pineapple, papaya and kiwi, these fruits can help you relieve indigestion. To be effective these fruits must be raw. Canned has no effect, enzymes are destroyed in the processing.

Herbs

Now a days herbs seem to be very popular. I'm not saying that I have used them or not or that I recommend them. But every major lab in the world including the USA is jumping in the wagon. I think that including some may be of some benefit for some of you.

Alfafa

The king of herbs. Full of calcium, protein, iron, B-complex, fiber and enzymes to help metabolism.

Cranberry

Proven excellent for bladder, urinary infection. Use capsules without adding calories.

Damiana

Another aphrodisiac. It is good for the nervous system, stimulate testosterone production. Very strong stimulant. Be careful.

Echinacea

Boosts your immune system. Resists infection, very popular to help fight a cold. Be careful with high blood pressure.

Garlic

Lower hypertension and lower cholesterol. Supports cardiovascular heath. Good.

Ginseng

It is used in Asia, China, and Korea. It helps the production of testosterone and helps the testes; stabilizes blood sugar, cholesterol and liver. There are many types of ginseng, panax ginseng China, Siberian ginseng Russia, American ginseng. Ginseng has a reputation for helping sexuality.

Ginkgo Biloba

A Chinese herb, which improves flow to the brain and the extremities, also good for cramps and vascular diseases. Some people get headaches. Be careful.

Golden Seal

Helps the respiratory system in combination with Echinacea . Excellent to fight colds and infection. Do not use more than 8 to 10 days in a row. Be careful with high blood pressure.

Kelp

An excellent nutritional herb, good for the nerves, energy, skin, and kidneys. Full of vitamins A and B. Norwegian kelp is the best and also is rich in amino acids. The late Guru Vince Gironda use to recommends, 20 tablets of kelp a day to burn fat.

Maca

The natural Viagra. It has been used for centuries to improve sexual performance. High in zinc, vitamins. Powerful for sexual energy. Check it out.

Saw Palmetto

Beneficial for prostatic hyperpesia, cystitis, low libido, prostatitis. Thousands of people are using saw palmetto with excellent results.

Psyllium

Brown seeds that encourage bowel's normal activity. Increased bulk to move food through the colon. For those who need a natural laxative, it is excellent. Used in many famous products.

Yohimbe

An aphrodisiac herb. Some doctors describe it for impotence. It can really boost your energy and sexual energy too. Be careful if you have high blood pressure.

Supplements

Antioxidants

Some antioxidants are vitamins, C, E and Beta-Carotene. Antioxidants are chemical compounds that attack a substance in your body known as free radicals .Many people, from all walks of life, are taking antioxidants. Very popular today.

Whey Protein

There are different kinds of protein, soy, beef, milk, eggs and whey. Some people swear by whey protein. Whey is easy to mix. In my top years eggs and milk was in, now it's whey protein.

Pyruvate

It is produced naturally in the body, it helps increase fat lost, so many bodybuilders use it now to get cut. It also will give you energy.

Caffeine

Bodybuilders use it to give them an edge during workouts, to give them a bust of energy when they don't feel like working out.

Conjugated Linoleic Acid (CLA)

People use it to help them gain size and strength.

Ephedrine

Ephedrine is extracted from the ephedrine plant. It is use to burn fat, also stimulates the nervous system. According to the FDA ephedrine has been implicated in some deaths. The FDA has taken it out of the market.

AC

Glutamine is an abundant free amino acid in the human body. It helps the digestive system, immune system, and stress, particularly in illness.

Creatine Monohydrate

It's made up of three amino acids Arginine, Glycine, and Methionine. Many studies have shown that supplementing may improve bodybuilding performance. Bodybuilders claim this is the most effective supplement for gaining size and muscle. It is found in red meat. Most bodybuilders actually are taking this supplement and most swear by it.

Desiccate Liver

Desiccated liver is beef liver concentrated by vacuum drying at low temperatures. The claim is that it's a high protein supplement. It's used to be one of the most popular among bodybuilders ten to fifteen years ago.

Yohimbe

It is obtain from the yohimbe bark plant. Most people take it to help them in the bedroom. A very, very, popular supplement today.

Glandular

Raw extracts of tissue concentrate from organ or gland of cattle. These include adrenal, pituitary, testicle, and liver. Bodybuilders believe, that it will increase their testosterone and will help them build muscle.

Orchic Extract

It is made from bull testes. Again, bodybuilders believe it will raise their testosterone.

Chromium Picolinate

It is a trace mineral and bodybuilders use it to burn calories and promote muscle growth, It also helps with insulin, one of today's favorite supplements.

Coenzyme Q10

An antioxidant, good for energy and memory, as we age memory diminishes.

DHEA-Dehydroepiandrosterone

A natural hormone in the human body. Excellent for the cardiovascular system, helps with hormones, vitality and energy. DHEA begins to decline in our early twenties and when we get to be sixty it's almost nonexistent. DHEA can reverse the immune function drop as we age. Be careful with side effects.

Essential Fatty Acids (EFA'S)

This oil is found in vegetables, nuts, seeds, flaxseed oil, regulates the immune system, has anti-inflammatory effect, etc. Excellent.

EPA Omega3-Fatty Acids

Are natural blood thinners, it lowers blood pressure. Helps arteries stay elastic and free of inflammation. Excellent for good blood circulation and finally it's a brain food.

Aspirin - The Wonder Drug

1 – Anti- inflammatory

2- Anti-pyretic reduces fever

3- Analgesic-relieves pain

4- Blocks formation of platelets in blood vessels

5- Prevents heart attacks and strokes

Some people take Enteric aspirin for the long haul. People take one daily or one every two days. Check with your doctor first for advice on this wonder drug. Excellent.

HEALTH FOODS

Health stores are a big business. You can find all kinds of supplements and promises. Sure there are good products out there, choose wisely, read the side effects and don't over do it. Make sure you stop using any of these products after a couple of months to cleanse your body, kidneys, etc.

Three Body Types

1. The **Ectomorph**

Slim, tall, long arms, almost no fat, nervous and talkative, eats anything they like.

2. The **Mesomorph**

Husky Muscular body, kind of athletic, very strong, big chest, very long body. Muscle size comes easy and progress fast on any exercise. We call them the fast gainers.

3. The **Endomorph**

Short neck, wide hips, and tendency to store lots of fat, pear shaped kind of body.

Three Body Type Goals

Number 1 - Add some body weight. Must keep working the big muscles. This body type will grow muscles kind of slowly and will take some time.

Number 2 - Won't have problems adding muscles. This body type is kind of bulky, and should pay attention to shape. Will grow fast.

Number 3 – This body type has high fat storage, will need to do a lot of cardio. Need to pay attention to what he eats and quantity.

ILLUSTRATION

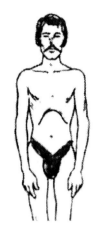 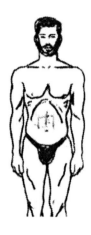 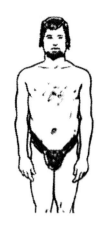

The Ectomorph   The Mesomorph   The Endomorph

Body Types

Probably you are a combination of one or two and sometimes even the three types. There are many different ways to find out which type you are. For example, there are height and weight tables. These tables however, only measure weight and don't look into body composition. Secondly, you can have someone use the skin fold measurement test. This is a simple way to assess body fat using skin fold calipers that tests skin and fat at various sites of your body. There's also underwater weighing, which is the most accurate way to evaluate fat to muscle ratio, however, it's kind of expensive. Finally, you can use the most common one which is look in the mirror.

Remember weight can be misleading. Two men can be standing next to each other and both weigh 195 pounds, but one is lean, trim, and very muscular, while the other has a gut that falls over his belt. Understand the concept? Body composition is what's important. This is your body's ratio of fat tissue to lean muscle mass. Body fat percentage is what bodybuilding champions really go by, and you should too, especially if you want to have a muscular kind of body.

A scale can tell you if you loss or gained 10 pounds, right? But did you lose ten pounds of fat? Did you gain 10 pounds of muscle? Female and males have different ways of fat distribution. Females put fat on their hips, legs, and buttocks first. On the other hand, males put fat first on their abdomen (The spare tire or love handles).The average guy's fat percentage should be around 23% or better yet 15%. Top fit athletes should be between 6 to 10%, sometimes even less.

Guidelines for Men

Nude Pounds   **Waistline Girth**
                                   Should not exceed (inches)

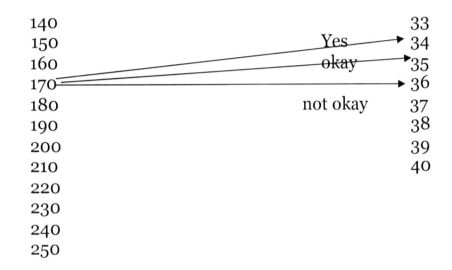

140	33
150	34
160	35
170	36
180	37
190	38
200	39
210	40
220	
230	
240	
250	

If you weigh 170 pounds and you can't get comfortable in a 35-size brief, you are carrying too much fat.

Body Mass Index (BMI) is the measuring of body fat based on height and weight, it also measures your fitness level. Sample guide bellow.

BMI	*Weight Status*
Under 18.4	Underweight
18.4- 24.9	Normal
25.0-29.9	Overweight
30.0 & above	Obese

Chapter 3

Exercise

The Super Tranquilizer

Evidence shows that exercising can help you in many ways. Check the following list:

1. More energy, better health

2. Stronger muscles, tendons, and ligaments

3. Clears thoughts and mind

4. Able to concentrate more

5. Improve your memory

6. Better self-confidence

7. A sense of physical well-being

8. Helps you sleep better, sooner, deeper

9. Fights depression and pain

10. 100% better body image

So what are you waiting for?

DELTOID

BICEPS BRACHII

LATISSIMUS DORSI

TRICEPS BRACHII

ABDOMINALS

QUADRICEPS

HAMSTRINGS

CALVES

Photo by Denie

115

Sergio Oliva

Photo by *Inge Cook-Jones*

116

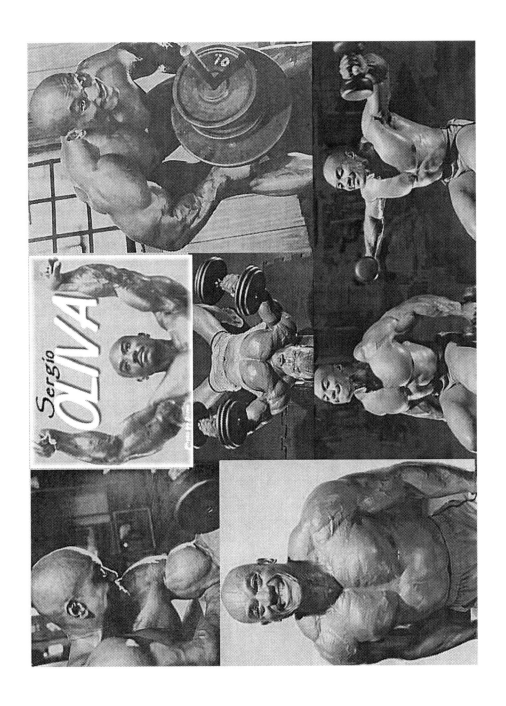

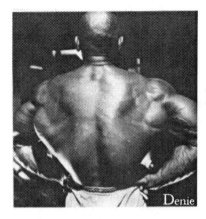

Back Development

Building the Myth's Back

A mighty back is a must to a weight lifter as well as to a bodybuilder. Latissimus dorsi (lats) means to me a big, strong, wide, V-tapered back. A back that does not have well-developed trapezius muscles is not a strong wide looking back. The muscles in the back are called rhomboids, trapezius (traps) and latissimus dorsi. Lats are the second largest muscles in the body.

Some people like Steve Reeves did not work out the trapezius muscles. Some claim that developing the trapezius muscles will take from your tapered or V-shape appearance, others do not agree with that. What do you think?

The job of the trapezius muscles is to erect your body and the latissimus dorsi (lats) for widening the shoulders; people call the lats "wings". The deltoids (deltoid is a word that originated from the Greeks) are muscles that gap the shoulders in a way that are somehow related to the back. There are also the spinal erectors, which are located at each side of the spine from the neck to the pelvis.

I remember when I would spread my lats coming into my 27-inch waist, the audience always went berserk. You could see the surprise and shock in their faces.

The widest back in bodybuilding

Don't believe that there is only one way to develop your back, you have to hit your back from different angles, and you have to shock it into growth. Include rowing and pulldown exercises. Also, don't forget your lower back.

Photo by Denie

The lower back is one of the most neglected parts of the body. In fact, low back pain is one of the most talked about medical complaint. Strengthening is not only a good idea but also a necessity. I think that the secret of a strong back is a strong abdomen.

The exercises that follow without a doubt, helped developed my back and if you give it a chance and stick to it, I'm sure you will develop a wide, V-shaped, awesome back.

A wide, strong back will make you look bigger and wider. If that is the look you want, then you need to develop your back to your maximum potential. Accept nothing else, do it!

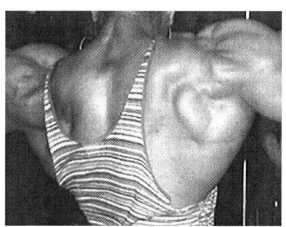

The outstanding back of Sergio Oliva   *Denie*

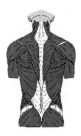

Back Exercises

Deadlifts - Along with the squats I considered the Deadlift one of the best overall body exercises. Bend your knees, then grasp a barbell with a slighter shoulder width, use an under/ over grip, one palm faces down the other faces up. Keep your back flat and head up. With arms straight and no jerking or pulling, stand up until your body is perpendicular to the ground, pause and lower it under control, repeat.

Palm –up Pull downs – (NOT SHOWN) Grasp the bar with the palms-up grip. Most people use the palm-down grip. Pull the bar from overhead into the chest around upper pec area, hold and return slowly to top.

Barbell Rows - It's the most popular and effective exercises to develop the back. You can do it with a barbell, machine or dumbbell. Stand close to the bar; bend over at waist parallel to floor with head up, row the bar up to the lowest part of your chest, lower the bar and without touching the floor, repeat.

Rowing Machine - Sitting on the machine seat, grasp the handles and row, contract, pause for a second or two and let go, there are many different rowing machines but all of them are similar and the concepts are the same. Very good latissimus exercise.

Photos by F.Marchante

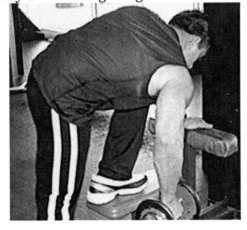

Low Pulley Rowing - Place your feet against the machine. Pull cable toward your mid-section. Making sure arms are straight at beginning of movement, stretch your lats. Good mid back exercise. Repeat.

One Arms Dumbbell Rows - One arm dumbbells are done the same way Barbells Row are done. Keep your free-hand resting on the bench for support taking the stress out of your low back. Raise the dumbbell as high as you can a little bit pass your torso, pause for a second or two. Lower the dumbbell all the way down and get a good stretch at the end. Excellent for the lats.

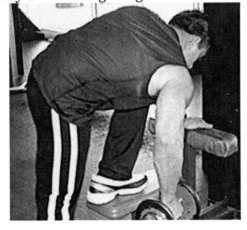

Wide Grip Chin to the Front - Excellent for making your back wide. Hang from a chining bar using a wide overgrip. Place your feet behind your knees so they won't touch the floor, pull yourself up until your chin is over the bar. Lower yourself under control to the beginning position, repeat.

Chin to the back of the neck –

Good for the latissimus to give you width. Same as chin to the front but instead you lift the body up until the bar touches behind your neck. Lower yourself and repeat.

T-bar Rowing -It is done similar to Barbell Rows. With one end of bar anchored to the floor, some people prefer to stand on a block to keep the plates from hitting the floor and stop you from getting a good stretch. Grasp the bar with one hand on top of each other or next to each other. And bring the plates close to your chest, lower it and repeat. This is a tremendous exercise for the latissimus, but also good for the rear deltoids.

Photo by Denie

122

Lat Machine pulls down to front - Sit under the pulley take a wide grip on the lat machine bar, pull down to the chest. Let the weight take your arms back to full length. Repeat.

Dumbbell Pullovers - Can be is done on a decline or flat bench. Good for the upper and lower chest, also good for the lats. Lie flat on a flat bench, feet flat on the floor. Hold dumbbells with straight arm position, lower dumbbells all the way back pass your head as you inhale, pause a second or two and return dumbbells back up as you exhale. Repeat.

Photos by F. Marchante

123

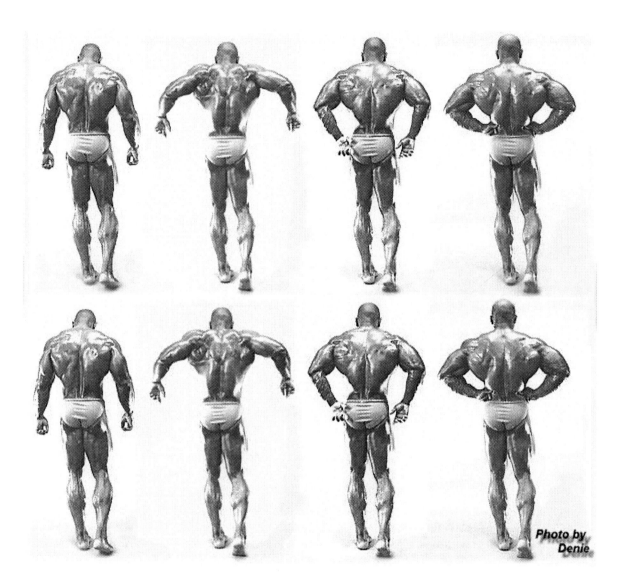

Oliva's awesome back development

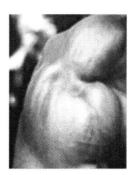

Shoulders

The Mark of a Man

Wide shoulders make a man. Nothing calls more attention than a man walking into a room with a broad pair of shoulders regardless of the clothes he has on. Shoulder development will give you an advantage over the opponents in competition as well as in your lifestyle. Steve Reeves was a good example of that.

The deltoids have 3 heads, front, lateral, and posterior. All of them must be developed to accomplish this goal. Shoulder width is hereditary, but this does not mean you cannot acquire a nice pair of wide delts if you work them. The deltoids (delts) help raise your arms forward, sideways, and backwards. The rotator cuff muscles lift and turn your arms. The trapezius muscles lie over your shoulders and back, its function is to help raise your shoulders.

When I work my shoulders I like to do presses behind my neck and do lateral raises to the front, sides and back. You have to attack your delts with brutal intensity, isolating the three heads, pumping them so you cannot even raise your arms at the end of your workout. You are after massive, outstanding, humongous, muscular, wide shoulders and you are not going to get them by being soft or doing light-weight exercises. Think wide, train hard, exercise the three heads, isolating the muscles and workout with determination and soon you will have terrific, powerful, wide looking shoulders that will make you stand out from the rest with pride. Let's start working.

Photo by Denie

125

Shoulders at Work

Shoulder Exercises

Barbell Front Press - Sitting on a bench and holding a barbell in front of chest by your lower pecs. Press upwards to arms lengths and bring it back under control. Excellent for front and side deltoid. Repeat.

Press Behind Neck - This one works the all three delt heads, upper back, the trapezius, and to some degrees the triceps. Perform this exercise in a slow way. Take a barbell with a shoulder width grip and keeping the elbows to the sides lower the bar behind your neck and as soon as it touches your neck, bring it to arms lengths. Many people claim this kind of exercise along with chins and pull down behind the neck cause rotator cuff damage. All of these exercises are just as good when performed to the front. Keep this in mind if you have rotator cuff damage. Repeat.

Dumbbells Front Raises - Holding a pair of dumbbells in front of your thighs. Keeping elbows slightly bent, raise one up at the same time bring the other down. Alternating the arms, works the anterior deltoids.

Frank Marchante Jr. Working shoulders

Upright Rows - Good for the traps, anterior and lateral heads of the deltoid. Keep a straight back during this exercise. Use a shoulder width grip, pull the bar up to your upper chest, and lower. Do not use too heavy of a weight to keep swinging to a minimum.

Upright Rows low pulley –Good for the traps, anterior and lateral heads of the deltoid. Keep a straight back during this exercise. Use a shoulder width grip, pull the bar up to your upper chest, and lower. Do not use too heavy of a weight to keep swinging to a minimum.

Photos musclemag International

Lateral Raises –A great exercise for the lateral head of the Deltoid. It's the only way to broaden your shoulders once you become an adult. It's Excellent. Arms bent at right angles, keeping the knees slightly bent, raise the dumbbell laterally to your side of the body keeping palms facing down, do not use an extremely heavy weight, so you won't cheat too much, don't use a jerk or the momentum to raise the dumbbell. Lower under control and repeat.

Dumbbell Press - Hold dumbbells at shoulder level. Hold elbows back. Alternately press one dumbbell up as the other goes down in a continuous motion. Don't lock out at the top of movement. Good for side Deltoids.

Frank working shoulders

Bent over Raises - Works the rear Deltoids. Sit or bend over at the waist grasping a pair of dumbbells raise your arms sideways as high as you can, don't lock your elbows, make sure palms are facing each other, and return to starting position. Repeat.

130

Lateral Raises Pulley–

A great exercise for the lateral head of the Deltoid. It's the only way to broaden your shoulders once you become an adult. It's Excellent. Arms bent at right angles, keeping the knees slightly bent, raise the hand laterally to your side of the body keeping palms facing down, do not use an extremely heavy weight, so you won't cheat too much, don't use a jerk or the momentum to raise the handle. Lower under control and repeat other hand.

Photos courtesy of R. Kennedy-Musclemag International

Chest

Building a Powerful Chest

When it comes to building a chest play it smart. You don't want to develop a big rib cage that looks like a bird chest and makes you look fat when you are dressed up. Yes, fat, that's what you will look like. The pectoralis major (latin origin) are muscles that cover each half of the front of your chest. These muscles turn your arms inward and pull your arms forward and down. Pectoralis minor are located under your pectoralis major it helps in keeping your shoulder blades down. Pecs is the word used when referring to these muscles. In addition to developing these muscles the serratus anterior muscles should be developed too.

What you are trying to accomplish here, is to develop your pecs. You want to add muscle where it belongs, not have pecs that hang or look big like a woman's when you're not wearing a shirt. You are after square, sculpturing pecs, and must develop your upper and lower pecs. Incline exercises work the upper pecs and decline work most of your lower pecs. Stretch and flex your pecs between sets. One time my pecs were so strongly developed that I used to place a glass of water on one of my pecs and the glass wouldn't fall and if you would stand behind me, you could actually see the glass sitting there.

When I do bench presses I don't lock each rep, instead I do a fast pace of short reps. I lock it every once in a while to release the pressure in my shoulders, and then keep going. If you work out by yourself be careful, especially doing bench presses. One time I got stuck and it was scary.

Don't lose sight, a strong muscular chest is impressive but always try to have symmetry, balance, and especially shape. Don't ever go after the big rib cage or woman looking pecs. I have seen many champions with that kind of development, and in my point of view, it's a very unbalanced and ugly body.

One person that comes to mind was Steve Reeves chest. He had impressive square pecs without a big rib cage. Again keeping all that in mind, you have to shock, and hit hard your chest. A well developed chest in combination with broad shoulders and a wide back is impressive. Let's work Sergio's way.

The Colossal pec's of Sergio Oliva

Chest Exercises

Bench Press - Use a wide grip, holding the barbell at arm's length, lower the bar with elbows away from body until it touches your upper chest or neck. Inhale on the way down exhale on the way up. The best exercise to pack massive upper body.

133

Parallel Dip - Chin against your chest, round your back slightly. Lower your body down and rise up to a straight arm position, lower and rise continuously. Narrow Dips with elbows close in will promote triceps developing; wide dips will target the chest. A great exercise for the pecs and also for the deltoids too.

Breathing Pullover - Breathing pullover is done after heavy squats. It's mostly an exercise for the back, but also expands the thorax and enlarges your rib cage. It also hits the upper chest and the lower chest. It can be done with a barbell or a dumbbell on a flat bench; across a flat bench or decline bench, do not use too much weight here. Lying down on a flat bench using dumbbells or a barbell at arm's lengths, bring it back over your head with arms almost straight all the way back, inhaling deep and exhaling when bringing arms up.

Incline Barbell Press - A great exercise for the upper body and front deltoids thickening. With Barbell at arm' length, lower the bar to the chest just under the neck, elbows away from body then push it back to arm's length. Again inhale on the way down, exhale on the way up.

Robert Kennedy

Plenty of intensity!

Flyes - Flat on a bench with elbows bent to take the strain off them. Feet flat on the ground, lower and raise the dumbbells out to the side. Concentrate to stretch your muscles. An excellent pectoral builder.

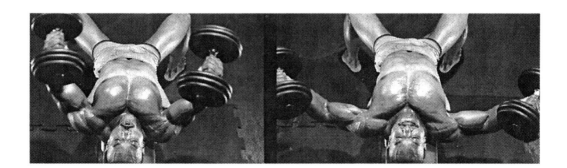

Peck Deck - Sit on position with forearms against the machine pads. Push both pads at once all the way where the arms meet, pause in this contracted position and bring the arms back in a control way to staring position. This is one of the best pectoral exercises.

*Photo **F.** Marchante*

Photo Robert Kennedy

Cable Crossover (NOT SHOWN) - Isolation exercise for the pectorals. Stand between two high pulleys, grasp handles with elbows bent around 30 to 35 degrees. Exercise must begin with elbows bending slightly and behind body. Move hands across the mid chest, pause, and contract pecs, then return to starting position in a control way. Repeat

Photo Robert Kennedy

Sergio ready to step in

Arms

Mind Blowing Massive Arms

The arms are the most exposed body part you have. To have impressive arms you will need to have mass, definition, and of course, peak. When I train my arms I like to hit biceps and triceps, super setting one with the other.

If somebody asks you how strong are you? What do you do? The first thing you do is show your biceps right? For as long as man can remember this has always been done. Biceps brachii, "biceps" means two headed. "Brachii" means of the arm. One of its ends has two heads, one attaches to your upper arm, and the other to the front of your scapula. Biceps cross two joints, the shoulders and the elbow, the biceps are used to bend your elbows and pull your forearms toward your upper arms. The triceps brachii is a three-headed muscle that works in contrast to the biceps. Its function is to straighten the arms.

To develop two powerful looking arms, you have to develop mass, shape, and definition. Always warm up your elbows. If you develop ripped arms your arms might look smaller, but they will look much better and stronger. It's better to have a well-defined chiseled 17-inch arm than to have a 19-inch fat arm. Beginners and most people spend a lot of time and energy working on

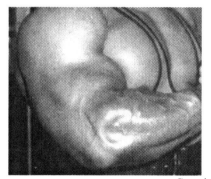
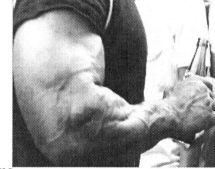

Sergio's Arms

their arms only to later find out their bodies are out of balance.

My arms got so big and so massive that I had to slit my shirt sleeves all the way up to my shoulders to be able to get my arms into them. In fact, when a group of champions went to Florida to train with Arthur Jones at Nautilus Headquarters, he measured everybody's arms "cold" right after we got down from the airplane and I was the only one whose arms were bigger than 22 inches, including Arnold, Casey Viator, Mike and Ray Mentzer, Boyer Coe, Franco Columbu, Frank Zane and everybody else that went. For biceps I like to do heavy curls, preacher curls, seated dumbbell curls and for the triceps I like to do triceps cable extensions, seated triceps extensions with a barbell and lying French curls. You must develop goals. You have to go after a super pump, isolating the muscles, hitting the arms from different angles, and doing different exercises to reach explosive growth. No way out, you have to hit your arms hard, you are after massive growth and sculptured defined muscular arms.

Some champions that had well-developed arms are Dave Draper, Rick Wayne, and Serge Nubret. If you follow my advice, you will be on the road to muscular, mind blowing arms. Don't be afraid, work hard and this goal will be yours.

Oliva's upper arms were Only 6" smaller than the circumference of his waistline.

Mind bulging arms!

Amazing size!

Nautilus Bulletin Excerpt

Chapter 36

The Ultimate Physique By Arthur Jones

To begin with, most of the claimed measurements are simply untrue. The largest muscular arm that I ever measured – or – saw was Sergio Oliva's, which, accurately measured, "cold" was 20⅛ inches. Arnold Schwarzenegger's arm was 19½ slightly pumped—probably 19 "cold". Bill Pearl's largest arm, his left arm, was 18 5/8 at a bodyweight of 222 in 1960—at the 1971 NABBA Mr. Universe contest in London, his publicized arm size was listed as 20¼, but it was obvious to me that his were actually smaller than when I measured them in 1960, and it was obvious to anybody who saw the two men side by side that Sergio's arms literally dwarfed Bill's arms, and now you know how big Sergio's arm were at the time.Casey Viator's arms were 19 at their largest when he was training in Deland—and were 18 when he first came to Deland, immediately after the Mr. America contest in 1970.

Arms Exercises

Barbell Curl - The most famous of all bicep exercises and at the same time the most productive. I personally like to use a very wide grip. I place my hands all the way touching the plates. Curl the bar up with elbows close to your waist until it touches your chest. Make sure your arms are extended at the bottom to start this exercise, lower the bar under control. Repeat.

Preacher Curls- One of the most Popular arm exercises also called Scott curl, because a former Mr. Olympia, Larry Scott, used it to develop his biceps. Place elbows tight on top of the preacher curl bench with an incline of about 85˚. Hands wider than elbows, and forearms should form like a **v** shape. Extend arms fully at bottom of movement, without jerking or swinging the weight. Curl the weight up pausing at the top before lowering it down.

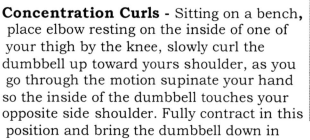

Concentration Curls - Sitting on a bench, place elbow resting on the inside of one of your thigh by the knee, slowly curl the dumbbell up toward yours shoulder, as you go through the motion supinate your hand so the inside of the dumbbell touches your opposite side shoulder. Fully contract in this position and bring the dumbbell down in as low, controlled motion. Repeat. Excellent for peak.

Alternating Dumbbell Curl - Sitting down on bench curl up one dumbbell first, and then as you lower it curl up the other hand alternating in a continuous motion. Excellent biceps builder.

Photo Robert Kennedy MuscleMag International

Lat High Pulldown Curl (not shown) - Sit down on a lat machine, hold the bar with medium width, keep your elbows pointing up all the time. Curl the bar all the way behind your neck, contract muscle, return to starting position and repeat. Good for biceps peak.

One arm reverse cable pushdown (not shown) - Facing the lat machine with elbow against your body, grasp the handle with palm facing up, extend or bring arm back all the way down until it's almost completely locked out, hold position. Repeat.

Lying Triceps Extensions - On a flat bench with barbell on front of your forehead at arms length, head held off the edge of bench, let the bar down slowly bellow your head, pause, return bar up with no jerking movement to starting position. Be careful with heavy weights and your elbows here. Excellent to add bulk at the top part of the arm.

Pulley Triceps pushdown - Grasp a bar with hands at shoulders width. Bend knees slightly, holding your elbows in close to body, press down, let the weight bring your arms back to top and repeat. You are pushing down instead of up which means much less aggravation to your elbows. Keep in this in mind. if you happen to have a sensitive elbow.

Photo by Jack

Photo by Denie

Bent Over Triceps Kick back –
You may use a dumbbell or a lat machine on this one. Grasp a dumbbell with one hand, bend over at waist. Keeping the upper arm perpendicular to the floor, raise and lower the dumbbell in a continuous motion. Keep upper body arm against your side or abdomen. Repeat.

Photo Frank Marchante

Parallel Dip - Lower body, keeping elbows close to the sides. Arch head forward toward the torso. Push up to straight arms. Hold and lower again, cross your legs at ankles away from floor to make it easy and repeat. Excellent exercise.

143

French Press - You can do this one standing, sitting or on your knees, with a barbell over your head and elbows stationary, as close to your ears as comfortable, lower the weight down behind your neck, press bar back to beginning position. Repeat

Photo: Denie

Forearms

Brutal Attack

Forearms only belong to a few champions. Do you remember the cartoon, Popeye? Good forearms that tie in with strong, muscular arms are what most people desire. But it is also hard to achieve. Forearms are a complex structure, that can supinate, pronate, grip, extend, bend the fingers and bend the hands into four positions. The flexor muscles are in the inside of the forearms and the extensor muscles are in the outside or back of the forearms. Flexors are muscles that keep one body part connected to the other and the extensors are used to move a body apart, away from the other.

Some people say that this is also hereditary. I'm not too sure, but I'm sure that it's a muscle that looks impressive when you have it. Some champions don't even train them. They develop their forearms from their regular workouts, from lifting, and moving weights, dumbbells and barbells. Mike Mentzer always claimed that he developed his forearms by training other body parts.

Not me, I believe in working them hard, shocking them to grow. My forearms got so big, over 17 inches, that I had a hard time flexing my biceps. Don't neglect the wrist because arm development involves a combination from the wrist, all the way to the elbow and up your arm. In my opinion forearms are like the calves, one of the hardest muscles to grow. Reverse curls is one of the best forearm developer as well as, the weight roller. It improves strength and muscle tone while increasing dexterity. You must develop and work in your forearms if what you are looking for is to have the strongest possible arms you can develop. Try my workout and see for yourself.

*Sergio **psyched** to do an all out set*

Photo Robert Kennedy

Forearms Exercises

Reverse Curl - Hold a barbell about shoulder width in a similar way to a barbell curl, only with knuckles up. Elbows close to your side, curl barbell up, lower and repeat.

Wrist Curl (not shown) -Sitting on the edge of a bench, elbows resting on your legs, grasp a barbell with palms up, allow the bar to roll into your fingers, roll bar back into hands, move the wrist up until forearm is contracted lower and repeat.

Reverse wrist curl (not shown) - Wrist curls with palm down works on top of the forearms. Same exercise as the wrist curl but it's only perform with palms facing down.

Wrist Roller Curl (not shown) - My favorite forearms exercise is the wrist roller. Hold a roller or bar with a hanging rope about one or one and half feet long attached to a weight plate, you may use a broom stick if you need to, extend arms in front of body, roll plate up by rolling hands. When plates reach the roller or bar, roll the hands the other way until plate is all the way down. Make sure the plate never touches the floor. Do not jerk the roller around. Keep doing it continuosly until you feel a tremendous pump. Take your time because many people can only do a few reps of this exercise, five or six pounds to start is enough. Keep it up and watch your forearm grow like never before.

Hammer Curl - Curl dumbbell with thump facing up, palms should be facing each other. Curl weight close to shoulder, slow return to starting position and repeat. Good for forearms but also good for biceps peak.

Frank Marchante Jr. Miami Beach, FL 2005

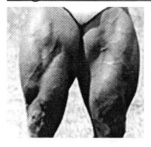

Legs

Columns of Steel

Built legs are like columns that hold a building; nothing will take away more from a body or bodybuilder than having a terrific upper body and skinny legs.

Have you ever seen people like that at the beach? People can either laugh at or admire you at the beach and for some reason, bodybuilders neglect working on their legs. They spend a lot of time in the visual muscles, arms, chest, back, and shoulders. The thighs are the longest muscles in the body. In front of your thighs you have a muscle group called quadriceps, people call them quads, quadri means four and ceps means heads so this is a four headed muscle. On the back of your thighs you have a big muscle called hamstrings then on the inside of your thighs you have muscles called adductors. The knee is the longest and more complex joint of the body.

Professionally there are a number of bodybuilders who have loss a major competition for lacking leg development. When training the thighs you must pay attention to develop proportions between your upper thighs and lower thighs. You build your foundation with squats, leg presses, leg curls and leg extensions. I like to do squats, using a 4 X 4 with heels elevated and going all the way down to about a 45 degree angle. I also do leg extensions for the front of the thighs and leg curls for the leg biceps. Leg presses and hack squats are good too. Always keep your back flat and straight when doing squats.

Tom Platz has one of the most extraordinary thigh development I can remember. If I remember well, Tom did lots and lots of squats. They call the squats the King of Exercises because it will make you gain muscle weight all over your body, not just in your legs. But here is another controversy, some people like the Guru, Vince Gironda said that squats would develop your waist making it wider and also develop your butt. Not in my particular case, I always used it and I loved to squat.

You have to work your thighs extremely hard but don't forget or neglect definition and symmetry always work all sides of the muscles. It takes dedication to build balanced thighs. Let's workout so the next time you take your pants off you blow peoples mind.

Oliva's legs were huge, define and powerful.

Photo by Wayne Gallash

Leg Exercises

Squats - One of my favorite exercises, the King of Exercises to develop the entire thighs but also the heart and lungs. Place the weight on the top of your shoulders with feet flat or in a two by four block. Lower into a squat position with the upper body straight. Immediately without bouncing, return to the top position. If you need to rest do so only at the top of the movement. Inhale on the way down, exhale on the way up.

Denie

Leg Extensions - With top of foot under the padding extend the legs and point your toes out .Do not kick your legs up. Hold the high position for 2 seconds, lower and repeat. Excellent for frontal thighs.

F. Marchante Photos

Denie

Leg Curl - Lying face down with heels under the Padding, curl leg up until the pads touch or are Close to the gluteus. Hold and bring legs down. Don't bounce the weight up. Work the hamstrings. Repeat.

Leg Press - Many champions use it instead of squats .You can alternate to squats from time to time. Personally I like the squat better for legs. Place feet on machine and press out until legs are almost straight, relax and repeat.

Front Squats - Good for the frontal thigh muscle. Holding a barbell with arms bent in front of chest, heels on top of block, squat down keeping the back straight and head up, breath in the way down, exhale in the way up.

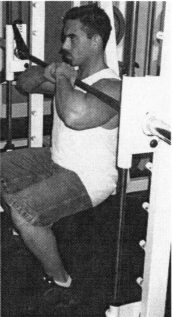
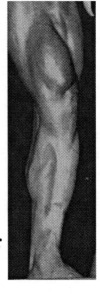

Sergio's Pillar

150

Hack Squat-Lower and rise by bending and straightening your legs. Some people believe in varying the heels positions. Experiment and find out what works for you. This is an excellent exercise for the mid and lower thighs. I personally believe the best of all leg exercises is the Squat. But try them all and see for yourself.

Calves

Powerful Diamond Calves

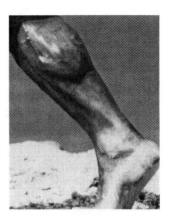

     To develop outstanding calves you have to do more reps than in any other body part. The lower legs must be worked constantly and progressively, you have to attack them like a vengeance or they will refuse to grow. You must exercise the calf until you are ready to scream .You must put pressure on them and stretch them between exercises to develop peak, it is also a good idea to walk in tippie toes every time you have a chance. The real name is gastrocnemius medial and has two lateral heads. The soleus and the tibialis anterior are also located in the lower legs. For many black bodybuilders it is extremely hard to develop a good pair of calves. Most of them develop what some people call "African calves", up high on the leg. But I have seen some black bodybuilders with terrific calf development like Chris Dickerson. In the beginning of my career, during one of my first competitions the competitors were expecting to see small African calves but when I pulled my pants down I blew them away. My calves came from my mother's side. She was a mix of moros and isleños, a specific area of Spain.

     In my opinion calves are one of the hardest muscles to develop. I like to do seated toe raises and standing toe raises changing the toes position. The trick here is to attack the calves, isolating the muscles, changing exercises to confuse the muscles, going after the pump, and doing burns with intensity. With determination, and extreme muscular hard work, humongous, and terrific diamond calves can be yours.

Calves Exercises

Seated Calf raises/machine

Sit on machine with pads or barbell on knees. Balls of feet on block, raise the toes and lower the heels to obtain full stretch position making sure to feel the stretch on your lower legs.

Photo Denie

Standing Calf raises/Machine

With barbell or machine pads on shoulders, balls of feet on block, lower heels from block and obtain a full stretch, raise as high as you can straight up with knees locked using your toes.

F.Marchante Photos

Toe Presses- (not shown)

Place the balls of your feet on the machine pads. Press with your toes; hold the weight for a second or two while contracting the muscle return to starting position. Not showing.

Waist

Trim, Leaner, Muscular Waist

This is the key to bodybuilding and to a great looking body, a small trim waist, with ribbed, sculptured, and chiseled abdominal muscles will give you an outstanding powerful look and a sign of vibrant health. Remember when you take your shirt off nothing but nothing, impresses people more than a muscular, trimmed, small waist. A slim muscular waist will make you stand out when clothed or in a bathing suit and give you an athletic appearance. It will make your shoulders appear much wider than they actually are.

Here we have another controversy, a lot of people do a lot of twisting with a stick or barbell on their necks or they do side bends. Some claim that these exercises are going to develop your oblique muscles, left and right side of your waist, making it look wider and fatter. Not in my case however.

The main muscles in your abdomen are called rectus abdominis, which means the straight muscle of the belly. These muscles pull the upper part of your body closer to the lower part. Oblique means slanted or diagonal, these muscles are located on both sides of your abdomen and help you twist and turn.

The secret here to a lean, muscular, washboard – waist is to combine diet with cardio exercises and make sure to balance your meals. Remember there is no spot reduction. Keep an eye on your diet. Let's keep in mind that weight makes a muscle grow so it's no different for the waist. I like to do sit-ups and leg rises to work my waist. It has always worked for me.

In my competition years, my waist size was 27 inches, making it one of the smallest or the smallest waist in bodybuilding, with a body weight of more than 235 pounds. If you really want trim, lean, sculptured abs you have to pay attention to what you eat and the way you exercise, no way out.

Here are the exercises that I believe developed my waist. Give it a try.

Sergio Oliva's abdominals were defined and deeply chiseled

Waist Exercises

Hanging Leg Raises From Bar

Hang from a bar with the knees straight and toes pointed forward, raise legs until they are at right angles to the body, lower your legs in a strictly controlled manner. Exhale on the way up, inhale on the way down. Very good exercise, not easy to do, it takes practice Lower Abdomen.

Hanging Leg Raises

155

Legs Raises

Lying flat on bench or floor, draw the legs straight up until they are above your head. Exhale on the way up, and bring legs down without allowing them to touch the floor as you inhale.
Excellent exercise for the abdominals.

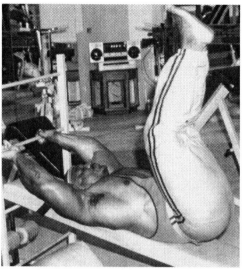

Crunches

Kennedy/ Musclemag International

Lying fat on your back, hands behind neck, bend legs at 45°, bottom of feet flat on floor, raise upper body ¼ up, exhale air, lower body down breath in and repeat without stopping. Upper Abdominals.

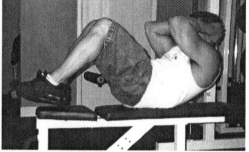

Sit –ups

I prefer to use a slant board on this one; you Can also do it on the floor, just hook your feet under a heavy object. Bend over at the waist and curl body up until you touch your knees with your elbows.
Exhale on the way up, inhale on the way down. Lower Abdomen.

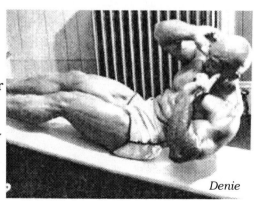

Denie

Body Twists with stick

Position legs at shoulders widths or you Can do it sitting at the edge of a bench, hold the bar or broom stick on shoulders, twist upper body to the left and in a continuous motion to the right without stopping.

Courtesy Robert Kennedy
MuscleMag International

Photo by Denie

157

Oliva's abdominal exercises

Chapter 4

Rest

Rest should be a part of any regular training. Over training makes you vulnerable to injuries and you will stop making gains.
There is nothing wrong to take a couple of weeks off, or go ride a bicycle or go swimming for a week or two.

Professional athletes learn this value early in their careers. When you go back to training you will have more energy, you will begin making better progress, and you will feel like a new person training. So plan your vacation. Plan your time-off, and then go back to your training with a new force and energy.

See and feel the difference. In conclusion, don't underestimate rest. It's as important as your regular training. Take a vacation or a good break from your training and see for yourself.

Maybe you will be surprise with your new gain, try it.

Courtesy Robert Kennedy
MuscleMag International

HGH

Synthetic human growth hormone arrived in the 1980's, no longer would it have to be taken from cadavers. What is HGH? It is one of many hormones that decline with age, like estrogen, progesterone, testosterone, melatonin and DHEA. HGH, also known as, somatotropin. It's the most abundant hormone secreted by the pituitary gland, sometimes called the master gland.

Human growth hormone is a natural chemical crucial to growth and maintenance of human tissue. Humans begin to produce growth hormone at birth and it circulates in the blood until death. It peaks during adolescence and drops every passing year. Many scientists believe it has to do with the aging process, loss of muscle tone, strength, increase body fat, etc.

The question remains controversial, side effects of therapy may include:

Facial hair   Cancer

Increases in LDL - bad cholesterol   Edema

Deepening of the voice

Allergic Response

Irritability and aggression

G.I. Disturbance

On the other hand, children lacking HGH cannot reach their full height and body potential. However, some people that use it, swear they never felt better. They lost body fat, improved muscle tone, strength and put on muscle mass like never before.

Others say it might make a dormant tumor wake up and grow. So the controversy is very strong at the moment even between physicians themselves. The amino acid l-argenine and ornithine can cause release of HGH, including l-dopa and clanidine. Most GH release happens during sleep, some is released during the day and depending on the exercise you do and your diet. GH may be released many times in a 24-hour period. However after age 50 not much is released. You can increase your GH release naturally by sleeping enough, using high quality protein and doing high rep workouts with medium weight which is proven to be better to stimulate the release of GH. Studies published in the New England Journal of Medicine claim that among other things, it will restore muscle mass, energy, sexual function, hair color, vision, memory and mood. The FDA approved growth hormone therapy for adults who are deficient. Exercise caution when considering using it. Be careful, stay away.

TESTOSTERONE

Recognized as a male sex hormone. Promotes sex drive, burns fat and builds muscle. Testosterone is the most GH stimulant of all sex hormones. It is the most important hormone involved with muscle growth. Today most men know that testosterone helps them with their sex drive, puts on muscle and will probably help slow down the aging process.

Baby boomers don't want to get old, do you blame them? Everybody I know wants to stay young as long as they can. That's why so many people go under the knife and opt for plastic surgery. All weight training is effective to promote GH release.

I've heard of many bodybuilders injecting themselves as much as 1000 ml of testosterone a day. That's crazy and very stupid. Of course everybody knows it will make you strong, but it's also a fact, that it will make you very aggressive among giving you other problems. If you are going to use it, do it with your doctor. Ask yourself first if it's worth it.

INTERACTION OF GROWTH HORMONE WITH OTHER HORMONES
Anti Aging – Growth

DHEA

This is a hormone produced by the Adrenal Glands. It diminishes as we age. Studies prove that is a promoter of longevity. DHEA is a growth hormone stimulant and also regulates insulin. It's called the mother of hormones because it helps produce other hormones like testosterone, estrogen, progesterone and others.

Melatonin

A hormone secreted by the Pineal Gland is the hottest anti-aging hormone in the market. It will stimulate GH release. The body produces melatonin only at night. Will help you with getting a deep and efficient sleep.

Thyroid Hormone

It also diminishes with age, regulates metabolism and affects every cell of the body.

Estrogen

Men produce estrogen in limited amounts. It is associated with secondary sexual characteristics in women and used as hormone replacement for females. Stimulates effects on GH.

161

Steroids

My book on bodybuilding wouldn't be complete without discussing the use of drugs. Anabolic steroids are a synthetic derivative of the male hormone testosterone. It helps the body retain nitrogen and enhance muscle building, such as growth.

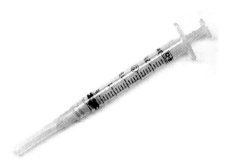

Most bodybuilders use or have used anabolic steroids. As a matter of fact, most athletes have used them no matter the sport they're in.

In reality I'm against the way people use them today. Kids walk into a gym and two weeks later they are using anabolic steroids. Whatever happened to diet, knowledge and training? When I was competing I did take some Dianabol and some Winstrol for a couple of weeks before a major competition and if I used them it was only because the other competitors were using them too, including Arnold. But we took them with control, in very small dosages, nothing compared to what people are taking today. Not even close.

Now a day, it's incredible the things that people do to get built. They are using pig drugs, horse drugs and this and that. My God I know of people who use more than eight different drugs, including GH plus about twenty pills of vitamins, two shakes and a couple of muscle bars daily, yes daily.

What happened to really working out hard? Learning? Diets? In the past champions took maybe one or two pills of Dianabol for two or three weeks before a contest and they worried to death about it.

I think the problem today is that a new bodybuilder starts to work out and he wants to have muscles right away. So two weeks later, he is asking about steroids to get big. He wants to have in three months what takes a couple of years to achieve.

Then the drug pusher sells you things claiming it's legitimate when in fact it might no be. You might be shooting contaminated oils, water or who knows what into your body. This is a very dangerous and risky situation. Today's black market earns millions of dollars a year. On the other hand, you are manipulating your organism and natural blood balance by using drugs to control insulin, sugar, etc,

I can't believe that people are willing to risk their lives or possibly even death just to make a couple of dollars, win a trophy or be in the public eye. This is getting out of control! We are living in a crazy world. No matter what some people think about bodybuilders, even with today's steroids and GH it's not easy. You got to work hard, make no mistake about it.

I hope that this situation changes for the better and people realize that it's not worth it. Look at champions like Steve Reeves, John Grimek and many others. They lived long and healthy lives. I hope people listen.

Amazing Sergio!

Steroids

Steroids have been around for a long time. Doctor John Ziegler together with Ciba Lab produced Dianabol in 1956. Later others Steroids such as Deca, Winstrol and Anavar were developed.

Common names in users are words like stacking, staggering, descending doses, ascending dose, tapering and shot gunning among others. A popular stack among many others is Testosterone, Insulin plus GH. In my opinion what some bodybuilders are doing is crazy, some champions are injecting many steroids, drugs and GH into their body, crazy very crazy.

Some popular steroids are:

Anavar	Sustanon	Primobolan
Maxibolon	Dianabol	and many
Winstrol V	Andriol	more
Deca-durabolin	Stromba	

I'm not going to sit here and lecture against steroids. I'm not going to tell you like other famous bodybuilders that I never took any, bull! Yes, I took some for two or three weeks, but always checking myself. I only did it for top competitions at the Professional level, only the top champions did it. But now kids, only three months into the gym are injecting who knows what into their bodies, taking all kinds of pills, growth hormone, and the list goes on. Some names I can't even remember or memorize.

I'm against the way steroids and growth hormones are taken now. I wouldn't do it, if I had to take all that into my body to make some money or take a trophy home. I would quit.

These people are going to have kidney, heart and maybe cancer in the near future. Like there are also some products in the market manipulating your insulin, your hormone balance, your pituitary gland, your testosterone production and this crazy list goes on and on.

What happened to a hard workout? What happened to a good balance diet and to rest and recuperation? People are manipulating, altering, and changing their body's' natural balance. They're taking one drug for something and another one to fight the side effects of shrinking the testicles, or to fight the side effects of an enlarge prostate, and so on.

What the hell are these people thinking about? They're spending a lot of money and taking the chance of getting arrested or be thrown in jail because it's illegal.

It's illegal, crazy, and stupid. I don't even want to talk about the subject anymore. If you are going to do it, think about it not once, but twenty times before. Weigh the pros and cons, think about the future. Is it really worth it? The answer is **No**.

R. Kennedy photo

GENETICS

Take a seat; let's talk about a fascinating subject, genetics. Everybody knows that in bodybuilding Genetics is very important to be able to develop a championship body. How we think, height, fat and muscularity is determined by genetics, by our ancestry or progenitors.

Many experts comment that I have the most favorable and best genetics in the history of bodybuilding. I don't know if this is true. I know that I grew no matter what I ate or how I exercised. So maybe, there is some truth to it.

In the beginning of my career when I first told people that I had only been doing weights for 5 or 6 years, they would get pissed at me. They thought I had been doing weights for 15 years or more. What would take a normal person to achieve in 15 or more years I did it in 5. When you talk about genetics who comes to your mind, Steve Reeves, John Grimek? Who?

Many other people with less genetics acquired great muscular bodies in the past. How were they able to do it? Keep in mind that this was before all the abuse and craziness use of steroids, GH and Insulin, but that did not stop them.

These days it would be extremely hard or almost impossible not to use **GH**, **Insulin** and **STEROIDS** to acquire a championship caliber body so that you can be able to compete in a top-notch competition against the hormone-drugs gigantic bodybuilders.

To acquire a championship body you will need of course more than great genetics. You need a lot of energy and plenty of time for an extremely hard and very long workout. You will also need a tremendous amount of concentration, super determination, commitment, and much more. Today there are also numerous kinds of supplements in the market to help you achieve your goal, some are extremely good, and some are not. I wonder how many champions including me would have looked liked if we had as many good products like there are now. Never let any of these thoughts stop you. **Train hard** never miss a **training session**, **eat balanced meals** and get **plenty of sleep**. Practice your **posing routine** over and over again and believe you can do it. **DON'T** ever accept from anyone that **you can't do it**. So the hell with it! **GO FOR IT**. Good **luck**.

Pain

Pain is the system the body uses to alarm you. It is the body's way to tell you something is wrong somewhere. It will not go away by working through it. Your body is speaking to you through pain.

Of course the day after a workout you are going to feel some pain in your muscles, this is ok, your muscles are growing and developing.

Dull Ache

This is the most common type of pain

associated with muscle strain. The

pain can go from low to a muscle spasm.

Sharp Pain

It could be serious and

maybe associated with

ligaments.

Pinch Pain

Nerve pain could be nerve inflammation. You could feel tingling, burning or some weakness. This is because of an electrical current going through your muscle and it is pinched somewhere altering the electrical current. Don't be a fool to work through pain. If it doesn't go away after three or four days of rest see your doctor. This is why I always recommend using correct form. Believe me it pays at the end.

List of main injuries

1- Muscle Spasm
Cause by use, soreness and tendonitis.

2- Tears
Rotator cuff injuries
Ligaments or muscle tears

3- Nerve Pain
Compression or muscle spasm.

Never work through pain, ever. See a doctor if you have any of these pains for more than three days.

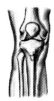
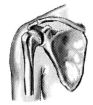

Bodybuilding Injuries

1-Elbows

The common name for this problem is called "tennis elbow". The muscle tendon becomes inflamed and irritated (tendonitis). In advanced stages, injections of corticosteroids could be required. You must be careful and warm up, be careful. Ice the area for the first 48-70 hours.

2-Shoulder

The shoulder is one of the most problem areas in bodybuilding. The shoulder is a delicate structure; heavy presses can cause tearing of the rotator cuff.
Again warm up, be careful. Ice the area for 48-70 hours.

3-Knees

Weight exercises have a heavy impact on the knee than any other body part. Squats without question are the most irritating activity for your knee in the gym. If done correctly, weight exercises can be used to rehabilitate knees injuries. If you are not careful, weight training can cause many knee injuries. Use correct form. Again ice the area for 48-70 hours.

4-The Low Back

Can cause pain, a shooting sensation, tingling, numbness and muscle weakness in the legs. Swelling and inflammation can cause sciatica, an extreme pain running down the leg. More permanent damage a slipped disk, beware. Apply ice for 48 hours.

5-Neck

Very vulnerable to injury, it's easy to get hurt with training, be careful, and learn to workout. Apply ice for 48 hours.

Mind Health

A strong body makes the mind strong.
Thomas Jefferson.

You must keep your mind working, stimulated, try reading books, learn about computers, socialize, go out with friends, and do puzzles. Keep busy is the first step to staying young, dance, laugh, travel, and have fun. When was the last time you had a good laugh?

BRAIN FOODS

MEAT

Meat is a great source of complete protein. Good for the mind, and building muscles.

PUMPING IRON AND THE B VITAMINS

Red meat is rich in Iron and plays an important part in building muscles and healthy blood. The B vitamins found in meat are critical for muscle building and energy. Good for the mind.

EGGS

One of the best and complete proteins with lots of vitamins including A, B-12, Folic Acid and Riboflavin.
Making it the best foods in the market. One egg yolk contains about 18 milligrams of DHA, and about 1 g. of Lecithin, 55 calories, 2.6g. of protein and 4.00 g. of fat. Keep in mind that eggs have twice the cholesterol of beef, so don't over do it.

Sex

Sex will do wonders for your mind and body. It's a great rejuvenator. A muscle will atrophy if you don't use it. Same here, excellent stress reliever.

Active

Keep active, exercise, go to the gym, run, swim, take a class, the mind is like a muscle, it must be use or will deteriorate. You are as young as you feel so start right now, go and have a physical if you haven't exercised lately. What are you waiting for? This is the reason you bought this book, right? So get active, **NOW**.

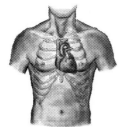

Heart Health

Most of you by now know that exercising makes the heart richer with oxygen, stronger and more powerful. Making it beat slower at rest and during hard work. Exercise is not only good for the heart but also good for the lungs and the circulatory system. Your heart is an amazing muscle. It's about the size of a person's fist. Your heart is your most important muscles. So take good care of it.

Eat less meat, more white meat, like chicken, turkey, veal, especially fish, fruits, and vegetables. Drink ten glasses of water a day, again lots of water. There is proof that a diet rich in fruits and vegetables can lower your blood pressure and bad cholesterol. Your total cholesterol should be less than 200 mg. Control your blood pressure, a reading of less than 140/90 is normal, 120/80 or less is better. Avoid as much stress or toxins as you can. If you smoke stop or at least cut down.

Sugar

A lot of sugar, smoking and a lack of a healthy diet with no exercise can lead to heart disease. Sugar does harm for your body by raising fat in the blood. It's also bad for the kidneys, and could produce gallstones by somehow raising cholesterol. Always read the labels, if you have to have something sweet try fruits, grapes, apples and pears. If you are getting ready for a competition don't use sugar. Please don't over do sugars.

Oils

The healthiest oils to use are canola oil and olive oils. People that tend to use a lot of olive oil have proved to have better, healthy hearts. Try it.

Fat

Not all fat is bad. Fat as monounsaturated fats in nuts, olive oil and omega-3 fatty acids found in fish & flaxseeds are good for the heart and support the fit person.

Fish

Fish is one of the best foods you can eat; it's good for your body. Some fishes are excellent sources of omega-3. As an alternative to red meat fish is really hard to beat. However, doctors think that because of its high mercury levels, you shouldn't eat too much of it.

Whole Grains

Wheat, rice and other grains are loaded with fiber. Go slowly at first, but in the long run it will do wonders for your digestive system. Fiber will help keep your colon clean, free of toxics and moving along. Fiber slows digestion giving you a sense of fullness. It is found in apples, citrus fruits and carrots. 25 to 30 grams daily is recommended.

Alcohol

Alcohol can raise your blood pressure. Try to stop drinking it or cut down on it at least by ½ of what you normally drink, if you can.
I know there are studies that show drinking one drink a day can be good for your health, like red wine, but don't over do it, be careful.

Garlic

Try to eat garlic every day. Doctor's claim that it will help keep your arteries clean and free of blockage. Some experts claim it will help reduce high blood pressure and help with blood cuts, etc. Give it a try.

Salt

Very important to the human body but the average American consumes too much salt. Salt can increase your blood pressure, promote fluid retention, etc. Use spices instead of salt, you'll get used to it. Always check the labels for sodium. Don't lose sight of this. Sodium is always hiding someplace. Look for it.

Stress

It would be foolish for me to ask you not to have stress. Who does not have stress these days? But try to control it, especially at dinnertime. Your goal is to control it as much as you can. Because we know that it's impossible to exclude it from ours lives. Try to listen to soft music, take a long bath, a long walk. Sit in a park. Have ten or fifteen minutes to yourself.

Exercise

Last but not least. Exercise is excellent to reduce stress, gives you more energy, can make you sleep better, and the side effects is weight fat lost, especially at the belly or spare tire. You will look better, will gain confidence, walk taller, and of course you will reduce having a stroke or heart attack.

Doctor's claim that in the long run, it will reduce your stress and high blood pressure. Plus it's a great feeling when you exercise. I love it. **YOU WILL TOO.**

"ATTENTION TO HEALTH IS LIVES GREATEST HINDRANCE"

PLATO

Air

Fresh air is very important to your health, air energizes and stimulates your whole body. Don't neglect this, breathe fresh air anytime you can, at the beach or at the park. Think about it, we spend most of our time inside 4 walls at work, at home, at school, at the mall or at the theater with air condition or the heater. When I was a child kids played baseball or others games outside but now most kids in the city spend most of their time inside with video games, computers, etc.

Water

Water a very essential nutrient. Two thirds of the human body is water. Men/women can only live a few days without water at the most. The amount of water the body loses from perspiration, respiration and elimination is about 2-3 quarts a day. Water helps cool the body down and provides the body with minerals. Not having enough water can and will cause many problems.

How much water you need depends on your size, a 180-pound person needs about four quarts or more per day. Drink eight glasses or more.

Water clears, dissolves, and eliminates toxins, relieves constipation and absorbs nutrients. The role of water in maintaining good health has been recognized since ancient times. Hippocrates, The Father of Medicine, recommended the increase of water consumption. Now there is evidence that cold water makes you lose weight.

So drink a lot of water, before working out, during, and after you are done exercising. It's necessary for all yours organs, don't neglect them. Keep in mind that enhanced waters with vitamin, etc are loaded most of the time with sugar. Drink more than you need, dehydration is serious.

Some Symptoms of dehydration are:

Dry mouth	Headache
Fatigue	Dim vision
Dizziness	Clumsiness
Fainting	Dry eyes

Drink plenty of water throughout the day.

ORAL HEALTH

Evidence links gum disease to different health problems like heart disease, stroke, diabetes and others. 75 to 85 % of adults are affected by gum disease and cavities according to American Dental Association. The Center for Disease Control indicates that people with gingivitis have a 23 % to 46% higher mortality rate than those who don't. People with Diabetes are most likely to have oral problems. What does oral health have to do with bodybuilding? I believe that if you want to have a healthy, greatly developed body you must take everything into consideration. What better way than also having nice, clean, free of plaque, white teeth.

List of some diseases:

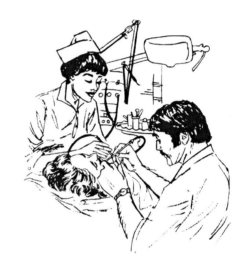

Gingivitis

Bad breathe

Cavities

Plaque

Tips

Brush at least three times a day.
Gargle with an antibacterial oral solution after eating or twice a day.
Visit your dentist once a year at least.

Worth Knowing

Absorption

The process in which nutrients are passed into the bloodstream.

Aerobic Exercise

Activity that relies on intake of oxygen for energy.

Amino Acids

Building blocks of protein molecules necessary for every bodily process.

Anabolic Steroids

A drug taken from a male hormone (testosterone) or prepared synthetically, to aid body growth.

Antioxidant

A chemical molecule that prevents oxygen from reacting with other compounds and protects cells from damaging.

Aspirin

Chemical name Acetylsalicylic Acid reduces inflammation and fever.

Calorie

The way in which energy is measured from foods.

Carbohydrates

Sugar and starches in food. The main kind of energy for all body functions.

Cardiovascular System

The heart together with arteries and veins transport nutrients and oxygen to tissues and organs.

Cholesterol

A fat substance found in the brain, blood, excess would give you arteriosclerosis and heart disease.

D H E A

Steroids secreted naturally by the adrenal glands in early adulthood.

FDA

Food and drug administration

Glucose

Blood sugar, major source of energy in human. Circulates in the bloodstream.

Hormone

We have about 50 different kinds of hormone. Greek word.

Human Growth Hormone

Hormone secreted by the pituitary gland, regulates growth, and is released especially during sleep.

Muscle

Body tissues made of fibers, able to contract, in response to the nervous system.

METABOLISM

Scientists use it to describe the chemical processes in the body, especially the use that involves nutrients.

Pineal Gland

Hormone gland located in the brain that secrets melatonin; it shrinks, as we get older.

Pituitary Gland

A small gland at the base of the brain. Supplies hormones that control growth, sexual development, etc.

Protein

Large group of organic nitrogen compound. Main building material for muscle, blood, skin, hair, and organs. The word protein means "most important." Hippocrates named it 2500 years ago.

Somatotrapin

Another name for human growth hormone.

Testosterone

Primary male sex hormone.

Vitamins

Group of substances required by the body for healthy growth, development and cell repair.

Insulin

Hormone secreted by the pancreas. Transport blood sugar into cell for energy.

Bodybuilding Language

Bitch tits
Female like breast development, also called Gynecomastia, side effect after steroid use.

Bulking–up
Adding bodyweight, fat and muscle.

Burn
Sensation on a muscle that comes from exercising.

Cap
The Deltoid muscle of the shoulder, which can be divided in three parts, front, middle and rear.

Clean & Jerk
One of the Olympic lifts.

Cheat Reps
When the weight is too heavy, some athletes use improper form to lift using momentum to assist in the lift.

Circuit Training
A workout in which the individual goes from one exercise to another without rest, thereby making it an aerobic exercise.

Cramping
Using shortened movements that cause a muscle to cramp.

Cutting Up
Stripping the body of excess body fat while retaining muscularity can also be called ripped, shredded, sliced.

Cycle
Taking one or more supplements or steroids for a specific period of time.

Definition
Very low body fat, other different names are sliced, cut, and ripped.

Flat
Muscles that have lost their fullness.

Forced Reps
Repetition of an exercise assisted by a training partner when you can do no more reps on your own.

Free Hand
Exercise using only your body weight, like a sit-up for example.

Glutes

Gluteas maximus is the short version for the human buttocks.

Guns

Name used when you are talking about biceps and triceps or strong arm.

H.I.T.

High Intensity Training

Intensity

Shorter rests between sets, moving faster or using heavier weights.

Isolation

Working out an individual muscle to produce maximum muscle shape.

Juice

Means anabolic steroids, roids.

Lats

Abbreviation for latissimus dorsi in Latin means lateral muscles of the back.

Lean Body Mass

Fat free tissue mostly muscle.

Mass

Refers to size.

Muscle Confusion

A bodybuilding system that is used to keep the muscle from getting used to a workout, by changing it often.

Negatives

Lowering away slowly.

Peak

Cutting body fat to achieve top muscularity on the day of the contest.

Periodization

The dividing of training length with specific type of training.

Progressive Overload

Adding weight, as you get stronger.

Pump

As a result of working out your muscles engorge with blood. It is a nice feeling.

Pyramiding

Increasing weight while you are lowering your reps on the consecutive sets.

Ripped

Very low body fat with separation and muscularity.

Rep

Each time you perform an exercise.

Set

An exercise that is repeated by a desired number of reps.

Snatch

To pull the weight from floor overhead in a single motion.

Press

Pushing the weight overhead to arm's length.

Six Pack

A well developed ab muscle. Also called washboard.

Overgrip

Palms facing your legs.

Undergrip

Palms facing away from your legs.

V-Taper

Big shoulders and a small waist, for example Steve Reeves.

Vascular

Veins that can be seen as a result of low body fat.

Workout

A training session.

Chapter 5

Mental Activity

Mental activity is needed to maintain, restore, or increase normal mental capacity. On the other hand, physical exercises are needed to maintain muscle tone and strength.

Daily intellectual stimulation is needed to improve concentration and mental capacity. Some aspects of aging can be reduced by a healthy life style, by doing flexibility exercises, mental activities, weight training, and cardiovascular exercises. You can slow the aging process.

At 60 you can have the body and appearance of a 40-year old person. Remember you are as young as you feel. If you want a more youthful appearance, strength, stamina, better sex, muscle mass, tone, better circulatory and respiratory system you know what to do. Exercise improves circulation to the brain, increasing oxygen; Glucose and oxygen work together in the brain. Exercise is the key to a better, long, healthy life.

Mature Bodybuilding

The mature bodybuilder should concentrate on lean body weight. He should make sure he does aerobic exercises two or three times a week to help lower his heart rate, help his circulation and to keep his weight down, also must include stretching exercises. It is important as you age to stay flexible. The census bureau estimates 25 million people are over 65 years old and by 2030 more than 64 million will be 65 or older.

Your training workouts should be intense and short, and should concentrate on the big muscles, like chest, back, legs, etc. Most people accept age as an excuse for inactivity. Most think they are too old to exercise. Not the baby boomers. They want to keep active, and young. This generation does not want to get old. Why should they? However take caution because a young male will recover much easier from an injury than an older male.

Everybody knows that exercise is good for you heart. Fitness is health and health is freedom from diseases, with exercise the heart becomes stronger, rich in oxygen, and beats slower at rest or work.

The best exercise is a continuous rhythmic one, which makes the muscle pump blood repetitively. Another reason is longevity, it is proven that people that exercise live longer and healthier, get fewer heart attacks and if they do get one, it is most likely they will survive it.

Mature bodybuilders should maintain a body weight for the rest of their lives. If you are under severe emotional stress, take a few days off, don't push so hard, and come back after a few days. Always warm up and cool down. If you have back problems swimming is a marvelous activity, also pull down on a lat machine, and avoid exercises that compress the spine, such as lifts and presses. Go easy.

Don't make your program so rigorous that you may get injured. The goal here is to get stronger, lose fat, stay flexible and be tone. Train, don't strain, and don't bounce the weights.

Stop or reduce smoking and control your alcohol intake. It's ok to bend the rules occasionally for a special event or celebration if you want to. Keep an eye on caffeine and salt if you have high blood pressure. Make sure to stand tall, chin in. Standing tall can make you look years younger and restore mobility to your body. A price of a faulty posture is loss of height, strain on the spine, sagging chest and more. Two of the major problems of aging are posture and flexibility. Another fact in staying young is relaxation. Play, laugh, it helps the gastrointestinal system, lower you blood pressure, among others things. A well balanced diet is also the key. It should include protein, vitamins, minerals, fiber and lots of water. Minimize sugar, sodium, try to eat when you are hungry, don't skip meals, exercise everyday, and sleep the necessary hours your body needs. As you get older you need fewer calories to keep going.

Exercise increases the filtration of blood through the kidneys and drain fluid in the process. It must be replaced, drink water, at least eight glasses a day to wash the irritants out.

When I'm talking to people the age factor always comes out. Again I'll be honest with you. I never think of aging. When I was in my 40's I was in much better shape than champions 20 years younger. I've used these concepts throughout my bodybuilding years and remained injury free. I still love to exercise. The thought of exercising still excites me. Of course, I don't work-out as hard as I used to during my competition years and I don't go to my maximum everyday. When exercising, the moment you feel discomfort, which is the beginning of pain, stop.

The Mature Weight Gainer

Don't force yourself to eat. Eat small portions three or four times a day. Don't over train or train for too long. Do heavy, short workouts, don't use super heavy weights. Use lighter weights, more reps. Have daily bowel movements. Eat well balanced foods, plenty of protein.

You may add one or two protein shakes with a multi vitamin and mineral pill a day. To gain size lets say you are doing bench presses with 175 lb 12 to 18 reps. You will not gain size like that, now if you add 20 or 30 pounds and do from 6 to 8 reps, now you will be gaining size. Keep adding weight.

This is the way to put on size. Eat whatever you can or want, keep track of junk food, and train 4 or 5 times a week. Stay with basic exercises, squats, rows, curls and so on. Limit your cardiovascular a little. Work your big muscles only, relax, and enjoy life.

The Mature Weight Reducer

Reduce the amount of food portion in your meal, eat balanced and quality foods. Eat a lot of fruits and vegetables. Eliminate junk foods like cake, desserts, sodas, candy, etc. Don't eat late in the evening, have one bowel movement a day. Don't eat everything on your plate. Share food when eating out. Do a cardiovascular exercise like walking, or bicycling, three or four times a week, at least half an hour. Don't diet; develop a long healthy nutrition plan. Take your time to reach your goal; you did not get fat overnight.

Degenerative Arthritis

To avoid arthritis you must avoid violent activities on your joints. Joints must be moved regularly, and the muscle must be contracted, thus will lubricate the joints and nourish the cartilage.

Exercise will help prevent degenerative arthritis and help with tendonitis. It will also keep your tendons lubricated and in top shape.

Joint Diseases

The symptoms of Rheumatoid Arthritis are swollen joints and crippling stiffness, more common in the hands. Doctors say that this affects about 2.5 millions in the USA between ages 30 and 50 but could strike at any age including children. It is more common in women than in men. By 2020 scientist estimate that 40 million Americans will suffer from osteoarthritis. The baby boom generation with many years of jogging, high impact aerobics and hard sports like football, soccer, etc. have caused damage to their knees and hips and are or will suffer from some joint disease in the future.

PREVENTION

Keep moving- Flexing joints lubricate them. Avoid pounding the knees, hips or feet.

STAY TRIM

Too much weight puts stress on the knees.

BUILD MUSCLE

Maintaining and building muscle helps stabilize knees, hips and shoulders.

WATER EXERCISES

Can help you move stiff joints without gravity-weight-bearing pressure.

RECUMBENT BICYCLE

This reclining position takes the pressure off joints. I personally like to use the treadmill.

WALKING

The best exercise to keep joints from seizing up, from the ankles to the shoulders.

LOW IMPACT

Don't do pounding exercises; don't put pressure in the joints, keeping ligaments and tendons flexible. Haven't you read lately of many past champions getting knee or hip replacements? Take care of your knees **now.**

Information

TENDONS /LIGAMENTS
Support the joints by connecting muscles and bone.

MUSCLE
Support the joints, and provides the force for movement.

CARTILAGE
It's like the body's shock absorber, made of protein, water and sugar.

BONE
When structure change affects the shape of joints and produces a breakdown in the cartilage.

INFLAMMATION
Toxic enzymes build up in the fluid of the joints, causing swelling.

GENES
Most of arthritis sufferers are born with genes that control cartilage formation and destruction.

Diabetes

Diabetes impairs the ability of the body to use sugar and produces abnormal amounts of urine. If a doctor does not treat diabetes it can result in death prematurely. A diet high in protein, low in calories and fat is important to keep your weight down so the amount of insulin you require is less. About 14 million of Americans suffer from Diabetes. More than 80% of heart diseases and 90% of Diabetes can be tied to unhealthy eating habits. There is also evidence that a diet high in fiber can help prevent or slow the onset of type 2 Diabetes.

Exercise is a must in two ways. It decreases the fatty tissue, and makes the body produce a little bit of insulin. There have been many famous and top diabetics athletes.

Circulatory System

Arteriosclerosis is a disease of the arteries. Atherosclerosis is fat deposits in the lining of the arteries resulting in, less blood flow. Atherosclerosis can be controlled by diet and exercises. You should also monitor your cholesterol and triglyceride. Hypertension (high blood pressure) can also be controlled with exercises. When you Exercise, the first effect is to raise your blood pressure but in the long run it will lower it. Another circulatory disease that is improved by exercising is Claudication, deficiency of blood going to the lower extremities. Every muscle needs blood in order to function. Doctors do not know how the body creates new blood vessels but it does, and that's what's important to us.

Stretching

The goal of stretching exercises is to keep flexible and to increase your range of motion. Don't bounce. Bouncing makes the muscle contract. You don't want this when stretching; this is the opposite of what you are aiming for. We know the importance of stretching in bodybuilding. Start slowly.

The Feet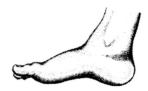

Let's no forget the feet. Every time I have looked at a muscle building magazine or book I have been surprised that none of them talk about the feet. You are probably saying, Why the hell the feet? We are not marathon runners. Without good feet we can't squat, jog, or run, for cardiovascular exercise. So I wanted to mention it briefly. The feet are abused day after day, especially by women wearing high heels.

If you want to be a top bodybuilder or if you want to be in good shape then you have to take care of your feet. The athlete's body is like a race car, everything must be working in perfect, top-notch condition.

Some problems related are Plantar Fascilitis, Achilles Tendonitis, calluses, ingrown nails, shins splints and one of the most painful and bothersome the infamous heel spurs. That's why you should take care of your feet, always use good exercise shoes. If you have diabetes you must check your feet everyday, this is a must.

Step climbing machine

Excellent way to work your cardiovascular system without great stress in your feet. You are increasing stress on your knees, be careful.

Cycling

A perfect way to get in shape for people with back problems. If you abuse it however, you may get pain or hurt your knees. Very popular now. Go slowly.

Treadmills

These machines are one of the best to get in shape by either young or older people. You can adjust the height and the speed. You don't have to depend on the weather outside or if the street is sloped or uneven. However if you run then you are pounding your feet. It's best to WALK, WALK, and WALK, your way to a trim, healthy person.

Paris 1977 Serge's Apartment, Denie - Fitness Photographer and friend

Sergio's drawing by
Bolshakova Irina Aka   Schneeflocke
Picture creation 1998 Courtesy of
http://schneeflocke.hu11.ru

187

FOODS

"Let food be thy medicine."
Hippocrates

I'm not going to sit here and ask you to eat skinless chicken, turkey or tuna. Something that I don't do too often. But it's good advice to keep in mind.

My personal approach to food and diet is a little different from other champions. I eat what I want, when I want. I eat beef, drink soda, and ice cream, but that's me Sergio. I know my metabolism and my body. That is why I keep telling you through this book that you have to experiment, try out things to see what works and what doesn't.

That's why I don't want to make this chapter difficult or hard to understand. I want you to use this chapter as a guide, not a bible. A champion doesn't make him an expert. Only you can re-discover yourself on this matter.

If you love beef, eat beef. The trick here is to eat a wide variety of everything including soda or ice cream. But never over doing it, keep control, and keep the portions small. The quality is what counts, be careful with the quantity. You don't need to eat like there is no tomorrow, experiment, do your own thing. Find out what works for you. Don't be conscious of restrictions. Your body needs different nutrients to keep running in top shape, protein, carbohydrates, fats , fiber, vitamins, minerals and photochemical.

The best diet for everybody including athletes is a variety of foods with portions, not too big. If you take too much you will store fat. If you don't take enough, then you will lose fat, just that simple.

What I wrote down in this chapter is mostly for the regular guy who wants to eat healthy, lose some weight or gain some, get in shape and obtain a nice developed body that looks 90% better than most people on the street.

Now, if you want to be a champion that is another story. You must understand that you must make sacrifices. You must eat a well balanced, strict diet, with low calories, low fats and include cardiovascular exercises to remove your fat from between your muscles so you get cut and striation. At the same time you have to get big without sacrificing definition.

It is not easy, everyone is not born to be a champion; you have to be born with good genetics, acquire the motivation and be wiling to do big sacrifices. Then you have to deal with the politics of powerful organizations. If you are really hungry, go for it. You may be the next Mr. UNIVERSE or Mr. OLYMPIA. Who knows?

But you must apply 90% of your time, actions and thoughts, you have to think and live bodybuilding. People like Frank Zane and Larry Scott did it and they were not born with such good genetics, so there is hope for you. Work

hard, read, learn, and find out what works for you. Don't let people tell you what to do, experience for yourself and discover what makes your body grow and get stronger. This is my advice to all of you from deep inside of me. Go for it.

I mentioned in some other part of this book that my case was a little different. I could eat and do anything; I never had to watch my diet much. In other words, if I wanted to eat ice cream, I would eat it. But I would keep track if a major competition was closing in.

Variety is the key. If you eat pizza and coke today that's ok, but don't eat junk food everyday. Tomorrow you eat a healthy, balanced and nutritious meal, this is the key. If you love beef, eat it; if you crave bacon eat it once in a while. It's an excellent idea to treat yourself to something you really want at least once a week.

Today you can find low-calorie, low-fat foods in restaurants, if you need or want to eat out. For example you can order a piece of meat, veal, turkey, or chicken with cottage cheese, lettuce and fruit. What makes a plate nutritious is not quantity or quality, but its variety.

As I mentioned before, I never really had to follow a strict diet and I never held one for a long time, either. Of course when I was preparing for a major competition I did diet some. But I could not be on tuna or fish for more than a couple of days, maybe three the most. I had to eat, steak and so on. I found out that even if I was eating rice, steak, anything, drinking soda I could get big and cut if I went to the gym and hit the weights with a vengeance.

I remember drinking soda and eating a steak the day before a contest. People did not believe it, but for me that was the way it was.

On these pages I will recommend what I think worked for me or what I think may work for you. Try it, but remember that everybody is not the same. Try and experiment different things. Use this as a guide only, not as a bible. What works for me may not work for you.

"You are what you eat"

Yes and No's

Yes	**No**
Eggs boiled, poached	Butter and pancakes
Tomatoes	Thick cream cheese
Low or non-fat milk	Fast food restaurant
Broiled chicken sandwich	French fries
Green salad	Pastry
Iced tea, water	Chips
Low fat yogurt	Peanuts
Turkey	Hot dogs
Lean roast sandwich	Second serving
Leave food in your plate	Pork
Shrimp, crab, fish, tuna	Fried rice
Baked potato	Egg rolls
Controlled red meat (some)	Tortillas
Pasta	Soda
Rice	Candy
Cheese (low quantity)	Pizza
Wonton Chinese soup	Nuts
Lean meat	

This is only an idea to keep trim and in shape. You can of course, try it out but this is only a guide. If you choose to follow this list you could be fighting artery disease, hypertension (high blood pressure), maybe even diabetes or cancer.

Protein and the Bodybuilder

Weight	Grams
140 lbs	104
150lbs	120
160 lbs	129
170 lbs	136
180 lbs	145
190 lbs	152
200 lbs	165
220 lbs	178
235 lbs	188
245 lbs	197
250lbs	200

The Big Four

1 - Milk and dairy products

2 - Meat, poultry, fish, and eggs

3 - Fruits and vegetables

4 - Grains, breads, and cereals

Denie, Sergio, Mr. Universe Dennis Tenerino and son enjoy a family dinner.

Tips

1 - Always eat slowly, enjoy your food.
2 - Always cut the fat out.
3 - Always eat balanced meals.
4 - Always eat fiber foods everyday.

5 - Always be careful with too much calories.
6 - 4 or 5 small servings are better than three big ones.

Sergio enjoys a meal with Mr. Universe Dennis Tinerino

Courtesy of Jack Merjimekia
Eating in a restaurant with friends Jack and Jules

Lose Fat

Here you're aiming to lose flab. Don't go by the scale. Go by the mirror or how your clothes fit not by how many pounds you lose, don't hurry either.

Cut 500 milligrams of calories daily, spread calorie intakes over several meals, include cardiovascular exercises two or three times a week. Don't overeat, leave food in your plate and don't have seconds, eat early.

Losing weight is hard but keeping it off is even harder. Only about 5% of the people who try to lose weight keep it off. I believe heredity plays a very important role in obesity. This does not mean you can't lose weight if you exercise and eat well. Today its a fact that the American population is eating more fat than ever before. Most of us watch TV after dinner right? So we sit for hours when in reality we should be taking a walk around the block for 15 or 20 min. This is a great idea for digestion and for keeping us trimmed. Walk fast then slow, listen to your body. Go slow but get out and <u>do it.</u>

Spot Reducing

Don't kill yourself doing 100 sit-ups a day. There is no such thing as spot reducing. You have to lose the fat with aerobics and diets. Then and only then will your abdominal muscles will show. The object to lose weight is to lose fat without reducing lean tissue something hard to do but harder to maintain.

This is increased with training. Forget the scale, look at the mirror. Scales are useful only to give us a general idea. You don't need a scale to find out you're fat. The perfect scale is your own image in the mirror .Your waistline will tell you if you are fat. Your weight could be muscle. You could be 170 pounds of muscle with a 34" waist or you can be 170 pounds with 40" waist.

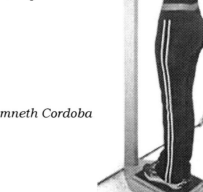

Jamneth Cordoba

194

Swimming Dilemma

Many people claim that you can't lose body fat swimming. What do you think?

Experts claim that the body retains layers of fat under the skin to protect it from the water temperature. However, I have used swimming in my preparation for contests and in my case, I have used it as a fat burning exercise. Give it a try and see if it works for you.

Swimming in my point of view is a great cardiovascular exercise.

Weight Gain

If you want to gain weight you have to work your big muscles, heavy squat, bench press, dead lift and barbell rows. Use heavy weights four times a week, rest. Take it easy; don't do cardiovascular exercise when you are trying to gain weight. Go slowly, you don't want to add twenty-five pounds of flab. You are after hard, muscle weight. It is better to put ten pounds of muscle in a year than twenty pounds of flab in three months. Increase 500 calories a day to gain weight.

Calorie-Expenditure Chart

Activity	Calories per minute
Running fast	8.90
Swimming fast	8.00
Weight training	8.00
Bicycling	7.60
Walking fast	3.20
Walking easily	1.60

This list is only an approximation. I'm including it as a guide to your physical activity.

Calorie Count

Calorie use in 30 min. activities

Activity	Calorie Use
Aerobics	210
Cycling	120
Walking	85
Jogging Slowly	270
Swimming	283
Rowing Machine	210

These activities were calculated for a person weighing 160lbs. So it will vary up or down from person to person. Use only as a guide to know the amount of calories that you will burn doing any of them.

WAYS TO LOSE

EATING PLANT FOODS

FAT CALORIES are the enemy. Eating plant- food is emphasized.
No more than 20% of daily calories should come from fat; the good fat, 50% to 60% should come from complex carbohydrate fruits-vegetables-whole grains.

LOW CARB

The number & type of carbohydrates are limited to manipulate glucose and insulin to lose weight.

LOW CALORIE

Eat fewer calories than your body burns to lose some weight.

If you like to eat out share a meal with another person or eat half and take the rest home and remember the secret to lose weight is portion sizes, you don't have to really count calories all of the time. I have never counted mine.

Remember that even 20 to 30 minutes of walking 3 or 4 times a week will keep you fit and will help you lose fat. The USDA recommends 5 to 9 servings of fruits and veggies a day.

Another trick you can use is to drink eight ounces of water at dinner and drink it slowly as you eat to fill you up. Eat slowly, give time for your brain to signal that you've had enough.

Researchers found that there are good and bad types of fat. Good ones are found in fish, olive oil. Bad ones are Saturated fats found in meat, butter, these are the artery cloggers. The U.S department of agriculture (USDA) claimed in a report that the calories we consumed went up from 3,100 calories per day in 1960's to 3,700 in the 1990's. No wonder we have an overweight problem today. At the same time The University of Washington in Seattle performed a research and calculated that a 150 lbs man would need to take about a million calories and spend about a million calories a year to keep the same weight. In my opinion portion sizes and common sense is the secret. What about you?

 # THE TRUTH

Here's the truth to losing weight. Eat fewer calories by eating less fat and burn more by exercising. In the Stone Age men killed for their meat, hunting for days and days, many times walking for miles across country. They had to work hard just to eat. When was the last time you had to work hard to eat dinner?

The consumption of meat, poultry and fish by Americans went up from 165lbs in the 1920's to 230 lbs in 2005. Experts say that Americans are eating about 535 more calories per day than they did in 1970. Every day 1/3 of children in America eat at a fast food restaurant, 8% of Americans eat at McDonalds every day. They eat 51 lbs. of french fries, consume about 600 million Big Macs a year and 20 billion hotdogs.

Forty percent of American teens eat no grains at all. 16.9 lbs of potato chips are eaten each year. 35% of Americans are overweight and 26% are obese. Therefore about two out of three people are overweight. Obesity is defined as being overweight by 20% or more of your desirable weight, increasing the risk of many diseases like Diabetes, Heart disease and strokes. No wonder there are so many diets and exercise gimmicks today.

The rules for losing weight are simple; eat fewer calories than you burn. Spread calories over several meals throughout the day. When it comes to weight control, exercising can take you far. You have to combine both, diet and exercises. The calories you should eat depend on whether you want to lose or gain weight. According to the American Heart Association to find out your ideal weight you should multiply your weight in pounds by (13). If you want to lose then subtract 250 calories, 55 % of your daily calories should come from complex carbohydrates, 25 % from fat and 15% from protein, sodium intake not more than 3 grams a day.

Stick with lean cuts, beans, fish, chicken, vegetables and plenty of water, Watch your calorie intake, burn off as much as you can by exercising. Keep in mind that light salad dressing is to heavy on sugar and salt and not too nutritious. Avoid canned food and frozen entrees. Never mix carbohydrates with fats; the key is to eat enough so you don't feel hungry. Don't forget people that eat 4 or 5 small servings a day lose up to 70% more weight than those that eat 3 big meals a day. People get confused with the idea of losing fat and weight loss. First you must lose fat and then you lose weight.

In December 2003 Germany researchers concluded that water consumption increases the rate at which people burn calories. Doctors from Berlin's Franz-Volhard clinical Research Center found out that men and women burned more calories after drinking about 17 ounces of water, calorie burn increases by 30% for both men and women. The researchers also estimate that over a year a person who increases his water consumption by 1.5 liters a day would burn an extra 17,000 calories, or a weight lost of approximate five pounds. More studies are needed to clearly confirm this weight lost. Remember never mix carbohydrates with fats and no sugar from fruits if you are getting ready for a competition.

'Your Body is like a car and it needs the best fuel in order to run properly''

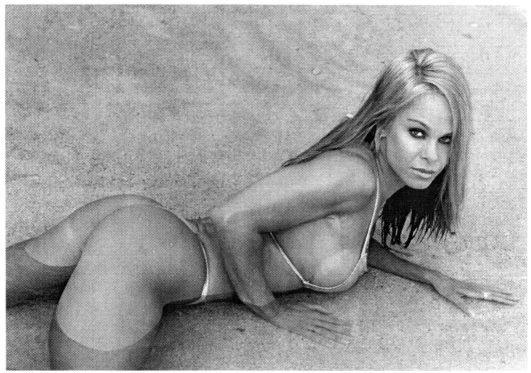

Beautiful Amy Fadhli actress and fitness model - photos courtesy of www.afadhli.com

Lisa Brewer/www.LisaBrewer.com

Jack Deeve

Serge Nubret- Mr. Universe
Mr. Olympus

Casey Viator - A true champion
Mr. USA – History's youngest Mr. America
Photo courtesy of www. Casey viator.com

Mr. Universe-Lou Ferrigno
Photo courtesy of www.LouFerrigno.com

Gorgeous Grace Rivera the Latina Diva-courtesy of www.Gracerivera.com
Photo by Frank Wood

What a stage presence!

Sergio Oliva-perhaps the greatest bodybuilder of all times.

Chapter 6

I'm including a list of Fat and Calorie Counts for your information to help you when planning your meals.

Fat Gram Counter

Item	Portion	Fat	Calories
BEVERAGE			
Beer (regular)	12 oz	0	148
Soda (carbonate)	12oz	0	152
Tea	8 oz	0	0
Red wine	8 oz	0	368
White wine	8 oz	0	160
Water	12 oz	0	0
BREADS			
Wheat bread	2slice	2.2	150
White bread	2 slice	2.4	72
Pita	2 slice	1.4	30
CRACKERS			
Saltines	4	1.4	32
Wheat	4	1.5	35
ROLLS			
Hamburger	2	6.0	320
Submarine	2	6.0	580
Hot dog	2	4.2	116
CEREAL			
Bran100%	2 cups	72	336
Special K	2 cups	1.0	222
Total	2 cups	14	200
Wheaties	2 cups	10	198
DAIRY			
Whole milk	1 cup	8.2	150
Low fat 1%	1 cup	4.0	110

FOODS	Portion	Fat	Calories
Burrito	2	19	414
Fried chicken	15 oz	42.0	825
Chicken salad	1 cup	42.4	570
EGGS			
Boiled/ Poached	3	4.5	360
White	2	0	34
Yolk	2	11.2	126
MEATS			
Sirloin steak	3 oz	8.5	199
Tenderloin broiled	3 oz	11.0	214
Porterhouse	3 oz	10.0	222
T-bone small	3 oz	10.0	211
Hamburger	4 oz	22	320
Lamb	2 chop	12.8	260
Bacon	2 strip	6.8	80
Ham fresh	3 oz	6.0	219
Spareribs	5 m	35.0	400
Veal lean	3 oz	4.2	170
PROCESSED MEATS			
Hot dogs	2	26.0	300
Turkey hot dog	2	17.6	232
Turkey	1oz	8.1	102
Turkey smoked	6oz	1.5	91
Turkey ham	4 oz	6.0	146
SANDWICHES			
Grilled cheese	2	48.0	830
Tuna	1	17	361
Ham& cheese	2	48.0	830
Eggs	1	12.4	278
YOGURT			
Low fat	2	2.8	220
Non fat	2	4.0	200

SEAFOOD	Portion	Fat	Calories
Bass	6 oz	8.4	300
Bluefish	3 oz	5.0	150
Fried grouper	2 oz	7	140
Broiled lobster	6 oz	7	220
Broiled Salmon	3 oz	6.0	140
Red Snapper	3 oz	1.7	90
Tuna light water	1.5 oz	3.5	65
White tuna water	1.5 oz	1.1	65
CANDY BARS			
Baby Ruth	2	12.2	282
Kit Kat	1	9	160
Milky Way	2	8.6	220
Snickers	1	6.5	130
PIZZA			
Cheese	2 slice	27	762
Meat	1 slice	17	272
PIES			
Apple	2	33	749
Key Lime	1	0.2	100
DESSERTS			
Chocolate cake	2	32	797
Vanilla	1	7.1	133
Gelatin	2	0	16
Ice cream	2	14.6	290
CHEESECAKE	2	14.4	268
Choc. Cheesecake	1	28.0	420
FAST FOODS			
Arby's			
Beef & cheddar	2	36	862
Roast beef sandwich	2	24	408
Potato cake	2	24	408

Burger King	Portion	Fat	Calories
Whopper	1	40.0	660
Whopper/ cheese	1	48.0	760
Hamburger	2	42.0	720
French fried med.	1	21.0	400
Chicken sandwich	1	26.0	530
Domino's Pizza			
Cheese only	1 slice	10.0	230
Thin crust cheese	2 slice	22.0	501
KFC			
Original breast	2	28.0	800
Hot wings	12	66.0	1060
Extra crispy breast	2	56.0	940
McDonalds			
Big mac	1	31.0	560
Quarter pounder	1	30.0	520
Fish deluxe	2	58	560
French fries	1 s	10.0	210
Baked apple pie	1	13.0	260
Pizza Hut			
Cheese pan	2 slice	20.0	540
Thin & crispy	2 slice	36.0	840
Subway			
Tuna	2	64.0	1054
6 inch cold sandwich	1	13.0	362
Subway cold	1	5.0	297
Turkey breast	2	8.0	546
Veggie Delight	1	3.00	222
Taco Bell			
Big beef supreme	1	23.0	520
Chicken supreme	1	20.0	500
Grilled sandwich	1	140	400

Soft Taco	1	10.0	220
Beef taco	2	20.0	320
Wendy's	**Portion**	**Fat**	**Calories**
Broiled Chicken	2	36.0	880
Chile small	1	7.0	210
French fries small	1	13.0	275
Grilled chicken	2	16.0	620
Fruits			
Whole apple	1m	0.4	81
Avocado	1m	27.0	339
Banana	1m	0.6	105
Fresh mango	1 m	0.6	135
Grapefruit	1m	2.0	75
Orange	2s	0.2	130
Fresh pear	2s	0.2	64
Plums	2 m	0.8	42
Watermelon	2 cups	10.0	100
Juices			
Apple juice	2 cups	0.6	232
Grape juice	1 cup	0.2	128
Orange juice	1 cup	0.5	105
Tomato juice	1 cup	0.3	43
Nuts & Seeds			
Peanuts in shells	24	18.0	200
Sunflower	1 cup	160	186
Pasta			
Macaroni	2 cups	0.14	220
Noodles	2 cups	60.0	922
Alfredo	1 cup	29.0	462
Salad Dressing			
Creamy French	1 t	7.0	70
Italian	2 t	10.0	108
Ranch	2 t	12.0	120
Thousand Island	1 t	6.0	60

Vegetables	Portion	Fat	Calories
Carrot raw	1	0.1	31
Corn on the cob	1m	1.0	120
Onions raw	1 cup	1.0	6.0
Broccoli cooked	2 cups	12.0	88
Potatoes			
Baked	1m	0.2	220
Hash brown	2 cups	400	640
Snacks			
Corn chips	2 oz	20.0	160
Popcorn	2 cups	6.0	62
Pork rings	2 oz	19.0	302
Potato chips	20 chips	16.0	126
Pretzels	2 oz	2.0	220
Doritos	2 oz	13.0	139

Health

PHYTOCHEMICALS

Are known as flavonoids, found in onions, grapes. May protect against cancer and other chronic diseases.

Carotenoids

Gives color to carrots and may protect against coronary diseases.

ISOFLAVONES

Plant food benefits may include lower blood lipid levels.

Approximate Calories and Percentage Fat of Common Foods

Chicken / Turkey	Portion	Fat	Calories
Light meat	5oz	300	30%
Dark meat	5oz	325	35%
Breads			
White	1 slice	75	6%
Wheat	1islice	75	6%
Dairy			
Whole milk	I cup	150	50%
Low fat	1 cup	110	35%
Desserts			
Chocolate cake	1/2 cup	225	90%
Seafood			
Bass	6oz	300	25%
Flounder	6oz	200	10%
Salmon	6oz	300	30%
Fruits			
Apple	2	160	4%
Banana	2	210	4%
Mango	2	135	8%
Orange	1	65	1%
Pear	1	98	9%
Watermelon	1cup	50	8%
Meat			
T-Bone	5 oz	400	45%
Porterhouse	5 oz	400	45%
Veal	6 oz	240	30%
Turkey Breast	3 oz	100	25%
Turkey Ham	3 oz	100	25%
Lamb	6 oz	325	35%
Pilaf	1 cup	225	5%
Ice Cream			
Low-fat	1/2	110	10%
Non-fat	1/2	80	7%

Diet-Sample

Muscle Weight Gaining Sample

Breakfast

- 3-Eggs
- Boiled
- Poached
- Orange juice
- Coffee
- Cereal
- Milk
- Bread
- Turkey
- Water
- Protein drink
- Light meat
- Fruit
- Cottage cheese

Mid-Morning

- Milk
- Shake

Lunch

- Light Meat
- Turkey
- Cottage Cheese
- Tuna
- Chicken
- Sandwich of the above

Dinner

- Grilled Meat
- Salad
- Grilled Veal
- Soup
- Bread
- Water

Lose Weight Sample

Breakfast

2-Eggs: Boiled

             Poached

Coffee no Milk

Bread no Butter

Water

Orange Juice

Dinner

Green Salad

Tomato

Turkey   > <u>Grilled or Broiled</u>

Chicken   > <u>Grilled or Broiled</u>

Veal   > <u>Grilled or Broiled</u>

Water

<u>Skip Salt</u>

<u>Skip Sodas</u>

<u>Skip Frozen Foods And Fast Food Restaurants</u>

Lunch

Turkey

Chicken Skinless

Canned Tuna Water

Grapefruit

2 Day Sample Diet – To Lose Weight

Day 1

Breakfast

Whole grain bread 1 slice
Light cream cheese 1 tbs.
Non-fat milk, coffee, or tea 1 c.

Lunch

Sandwich lean ham 1 med.
Fresh fruit 1 med.
Coffee, water 8 oz.

Dinner
Chicken breast broiled 1 sm.
Rice 1 cup
Fruits 1 sm.
Coffee, water 8 oz.

Day 2

Breakfast

Bran cake 1 sm.
Orange juice 6 oz.
Coffee, tea, water 8oz.

Lunch

 Turkey sandwich 1 med.
Fresh fruit 1 med.
Juice, water, coffee 8 oz.

Dinner
Vegetable salad 1 med.
reduced fat dressing 2 tbs.
Whole grain bread 1 slice
Tomatoes 1 or 2
Coffe, water 8 oz.

F.Marchante

1-DAY SAMPLE CALORIE COUNT

(TO LOSE)

MEAL	CALORIES
BREAKFAST	
Banana 1 sm.	118
Non fat milk or coffee 6oz	150
Eggs poached 2	240
Wheat toast 1 slice	70
8oz Water	0
Total	578

LUNCH	
Turkey sandwich 1 sm.	250
Carrot 1 sm.	40
Yogurt 1 sm.	150
Water 8 oz	0
Total	440

SNACK	CALORIES
Calories	
Apple 1 sm.	100

DINNER	
Grilled turkey sandwich 1 med.	250
Wheat toast 1 slice	70
Pear 1 sm.	120
Water 8 oz	0
	540
Total	1,558

A pound of fat approximately is about 3,500 calories if you follow a diet similar to the one above and you exercise 3 or 4 times a week you should lose a good amount of weight- fat every month, adding a respectable amount of weight loss if you keep it for least say 6 months to a year. Every week or ten days take a break and eat all you want. This way is easier and you have something to look forward to.

The Myth's Lean Sample Menus

DAY 1

Breakfast

Coffee 1 sm.

Banana 1 sm.

Cup skim milk 6 oz

Water 8oZ

Snack

Yogurt 1 sm.

Water 8oz

Lunch

Turkey sandwich 1 med.

Fruit 1 or 2 sm.

Water 8 oz

Snack

Carrot 1 sm.

Dinner

Grilled fish 1 med.

Cole slaw 1 cup

Water 8oz

DAY 2

Breakfast

Poached eggs 1 or 2

Wheat toast 1 slice

Coffee or orange juice sm.

Water 8 oz

Snack

Fresh fruit 1 sm.

Water 8 oz

Lunch

Tuna sandwich 1 med.

Water 8oz

Energy bar or skim milk sm.

Dinner

Grilled chicken med.

Vegetables 1 cup

Dry toast 1 slice

Water 8 oz

Lean Menus

DAY 3

Breakfast

Bran flakes 1cup

Coffee or skim milk sm.

Water 8oz

Snack

Fruit 1 sm.

Water 8oz

Lunch

Turkey sandwich 1 med.

Yogurt 1 sm.

Skim milk 6 oz

Water 8oz

Dinner

Grilled veal med.

Vegetables 1 cup

Skim milk 6 oz

Water 8 oz

DAY4

Breakfast

Wheat biscuits 2 sm.

Banana 1 sm.

Coffee or skim milk sm.

Water 8 oz

Snack

Fruit 1 sm.

Lunch

Small tuna sandwich/Salmon

Carrot 1 sm.

Coffee or skim milk sm.

Water 8oz

Snack

Yogurt 1 sm.

Dinner

Small grilled steak

Baked potato 1 sm.

Vegetables 1 cup

Water 8 oz

Cut or Eliminate

Refined Sugars and Flours

White refined sugar, avoid sugar substitute, saccharin, cyclamate.
Such as cookies, pastry, cakes.

Fat

Those found in red meat and unpreserved vegetable oils are the worst.

Frozen Dinners

Preservatives, additives , sodium

Dessert

Processed sugar desserts.

Canned Vegetables and Processed Meats

Canned fruits and vegetables.

Hot dogs and luncheon meats preserved with preservatives.

Increase

Whole Grain

Bran, whole grain cereals , bread.

Wheat Germ

Loaded with Vitamin E, Folic Acid, and Magnesium, traces minerals, iron and zinc.

Seafood

Salmon, tuna, any fish is good.

Eggs

They are a good source of protein; they have a bad reputation over cholesterol.

Yogurt

Loaded with nutrition and active cultures for good digestion.

Nuts and Seeds

Cashews, pumpkin, sunflower, almonds (unsalted)

Vegetable

Green vegetables - broccoli.

Beverage

Fruit, vegetable, juices (no sugar), non-fat milk, water.
Make sure to stay away from salty foods, sugar, also make sure the meat you eat is lean meat and cut off as much fat as possible. Drink plenty of water

Restaurant Smarts

The average American eats out three or four times a week, probably one meal a day is in a fast food restaurant.
Here are some ideas to use when eating out the next time.

Breakfast

Fruit 1

Bagel 1

Cereal 1

Eggs

Poached/Boiled 1 or 2

Egg Whites 2 or 3

Non-fat yogurt

Coffee/non- fat milk

Water 8 oz

Limit Foods

Omelet 1/2

Ham 1

Sausage 1

Hash Brown

Whole milk

Lunch or Dinner

Broiled or Grilled

Fish 1

Tuna 1 Snapper 1

Broiled chicken

Turkey

Filet mignon (small)

Side Dish

Pasta with tomato sauce 1

White rice 1 cup

Water 8 oz

Limit Foods

Prime ribs 1 or 2

Spare ribs 1 or 2

Ham 1

 Meat/ gravy 1 or 2

Fried chicken 1

Hamburgers 1

Hot dogs / sausages 1 or 2

Chinese Restaurant

Try these:

Egg flower 1

Wonton 1

Sizzling rice 1 cup

Sum 1

Broiled/ steamed fish 1

Kung Pao chicken 1

White rice 1 cup

Chicken and vegetables 1

Beef with vegetables 1

Water 8 oz

Italian Restaurants

Steamed clams 1

Minestrone 1

Pasta & Forgiale soup

Consommé 1

House salad 1

Steamed vegetables 1

Cervichi 1

Snapper/ bass 1

Breast of chicken 1

Broiled chicken 1

Medallions of lamb 1

Veal piccata 1

Vermicelli 1

Fettuccine 1

Spaghetti with tomato 1

Vegetarian lasagna 1

Vegetarian pizza 1

Water 8 oz

Desserts

Meringue 1

Latin Restaurants

When eating Cuban or Puerto Rican foods try some of these:

Café con leche 8 oz

Expresso 1

Black beans 1 cup

Orange juice 8 oz

Cuban bread- no butter

Tropical fruits –

White rice 1 cup 1

mangos – guava

Fufu 1 cup

Water 8 oz

ESPRESSO: Ah, cafecito cubano! It runs through the veins of Cubans everywhere. Good at any time. It increases the metabolism so that you burn more calories.

Arroz con Pollo

Main Dishes

Carne Asada (broiled beef) 1

Arroz con Pollo (chicken and yellow rice)

Tasajo with rice 1 cup each

Pollo asado

Fast Foods

Subway

Veggie delight 1

Turkey breast 1

Turkey breast & ham 1

Subway club 1

Roasted chicken breast 1

Water 8 oz

Burger King

Chicken sandwich 1

Chicken whopper 1

Whopper Jr. 1

Whopper- (take out the bread) 1

Chicken nuggets 8

Diet soda (small glass)

Water 8 oz

McDonald's

Chicken sandwich grilled 1

Chicken sandwich 1

Salad 1

Big Mac (take the bread out) 1

Chicken nuggets

Orange juice 8 oz

Diet soda (small glass)

Water 8 oz

Wendy's

Chicken sandwich 1

Chicken salad 1

Green salad 1

Diet soda (small glass)

Water 8 oz

Women

     I don't like to talk about women but sometimes I have to. Women are one of God's most beautiful creations. To begin with I don't like to go out with a very muscular woman. So muscular that people wouldn't be able to tell who is the man, she or me? I like a woman who keeps in shape maybe does aerobics or some kind of lightweight training. Somebody that is trim, in shape, and well proportioned. But most of all, somebody that is beautiful inside, and has a sense of humor and of course likes music and dancing like I do. She will also have to understand my true love is my son and daughter and of course, my love to train at the gym.

     Like any other man I have some stories to tell. Things that happen to each and every one of us as we grow older and the years pass by, we look back and sometimes we just have to laugh. Sometimes we get sad or even wonder what could have been.

     I'm going to share two incidents with you. One time I was in Europe and I came back to the hotel room right after a competition and as everybody that has been in one knows how tire and exhausted you finish that night. The hard months of training, the diets, the sweating, and the stress takes it toll. I got to my room and took a shower and when I came out of the shower, Lord have Mercy, I almost died of a heart attack! Somehow a beautiful lady had sneaked into my room and was hiding under my bed, she said, "I have to have you". Wow! I was in my late thirties, in great shape, full of hormones, and in a lot of magazines at that time.

     Another story that I would like to share with all of you is when one day I was in a competition and a young lady came looking for me with a gun. Hmm.For some reason I don't remember now if she was jealous. I had to escape through the backdoor in a hurry.

     As all of you might know, I was married once with a Mexican lady. I had two daughters, and divorced. Got married a second time, to an American woman, Arlene, and I had my son Sergio Jr. 21, and Julia 18. I divorced some years ago.

Amy Limas 2004 2nd WNBF
Figure Championship
Photo by Lisa Brewer

Photo by Lisa Brewer

Jennifer Bishop WNBF 2004 4th Pro natural Atlantic Coast Figure Championship

Women Training

Most women don't like to train hard because they believe they will develop men like muscular bodies. Women have much less testosterone than men do. A woman with normal hormones will always appear feminine, so it's nearly impossible to get as much muscle as men do. Exercises will only help her by improving her overall appearance. The cosmetic training effects will make her legs firmer, her waist smaller ect. When exercising and training, I think a woman should concentrate in staying trim, flexible, attractive, sexy and healthy. Naturally the approach is different; the basic exercises are the same. Achieve this kind of body by doing aerobic exercises like walking, jogging and stretching to keep flexible, young looking, and your cardiovascular system in top shape. Uplift your bust, get shapely shoulders, put on some lean body weight or for the overweight woman lose weight. Use light or medium weights to keep tone and strong especially in the legs and arms were women develop problems especially. My personal opinion is if I'm walking beside a woman there should be no doubt about who the man is.

Is hard for a woman to achieve and maintain a lean trim body, don't lose sight of what you eat, eat well balanced meals, four or five small portions is better to get lean. Cut the fat out and keep portions small, don't eat too late at night. Drink eight glasses of water a day or more, stay away from the sun or use sun protection.

Cellulite:
95% of women have some cellulite on their bodies. Very rarely does it appear in men.

Cellulite loves:

Setting around
Processed & refined foods
Coffee
Alcohol
Neglecting one's body

Cellulite hates:
Exercise
Low fat diet
Lots of water

There is no reason why you too can't develop a trim, sexy, healthy looking body. I have helped train many beautiful women and I found out what works better for them. So follow my workout, never, never go for a muscular body, but go after a beautiful trim sexy and strong body. Never workout alone for safety reasons, if you don't feel good one day, skip it, take a break come back next time with more desire to train.

Follow my routine below but from time to time change it, experiment different routines, try new exercises, high reps, low reps, faster, don't be afraid, watch what you eat but don't be a slave counting calories, learn to eat. Do your homework. Let's do it, **now.**

Women Workout

Warm-up

You can do jumping jacks, run in place or do the dumbbell swing.

1- Dumbbell swing - With dumbbell between your legs, hold it with two hands and swing it up & down for 8 or 10 reps. Excellent warm-up.

2- Straight leg kick -Face down on bench

    Hips & thighs
  Lift one leg with toe pointing backward as high as you can do 8 or 10 reps.

3- Straight leg kick to side

  Hips & thighs
  Lying on your side raise your leg as far to the side as you can, toe pointing upward. Do 8 or 10 reps each side.

4- Leg raise on bench

  Lower abdomen
  Flat on a bench only to about the hips. Hold the sides of the bench and raise
  your legs until they are straight up. Lower them to about 1 or 2 inches
  but do not touch the floor, keep the tension on the abdomen muscle, go up
  and down for 8 or 10 reps.

5 - Kneeling back kicks

  Hips, Waist & lower back
Get down on four, pick one knee and draw it forward toward your chin, bring your head down as if they were going to meet, then extend same leg backward and at the same time bring up your head. Repeat with each leg for 8 or 10 reps.
  These are not only good warm-ups but also good exercises for the abdomen & legs.

Grace Rivera –The Latina Diva/www.Gracerivera.com

Basic Routines

Lose body fat and gain muscle with three workouts a week.

Warm-up

Dumbbells swing, treadmill walking.

Toe touching

Abdomen

Crunches sit-ups	3 sets /8 reps
Kneeling back kicks	3 sets/8 reps

Chest/Pecs

Bench press	3 sets/8reps
Flyes/ peck deck	3 sets/8 reps

Shoulders

Dumbbell Lateral raises	3 sets/8reps
Dumbbell Front raises	3 sets/8 reps

Back

Barbell rows	3 sets/8 reps

Arms

Barbell/Dumbbell Curls	3 sets/ 8 reps
Triceps press down	3 sets/ 8 reps

Lisa Brewer

Legs/thighs

Squat	3 sets/8 reps
Leg extensions	3 sets /8reps

Calves

Toe Raises   3 sets /8reps   *Jamneth Cordoba*

Start   **Finish**

Aerobic exercises are done on the same days or even better on alternate days. After 3 months you can move to the intermediate routine.

Intermediate Routine

Warm-up

Dumbbells swing, treadmill walking

Abdomen (not shown)

Crunches sit-ups   3 sets /8 reps

Kneeling back kicks   3 sets/8 reps

 Side leg kicks   3 sets/8 reps

Jamneth Cordoba

Chest/pecs (not shown)

Bench press   3 sets/8reps

Flyes/ peck deck   3 sets/8 reps

Shoulders

Dumbbell Lateral raises   3 sets/8reps

Dumbbell Front raises   3 sets/8 reps

Bent over Laterals raises   3 sets/8 reps

 Dumbbell Press   3 sets/8 reps

Dumbbell Press

Dumbbell Lateral raises

Finish

Start

Arms

Barbell /dumbbell curls	3 sets/ 8 reps
Preacher Curls	3 sets/ 8 reps
Lat Triceps pushdown	3 sets/ 8 reps

Barbell curls

Lisa Brewer

Preacher Curls

Start   **Finish**

Triceps pushdown

Start   *Finish*

Beautiful Jamneth Cordoba working out triceps

Back

Dumbbells rows	3 sets /8reps
Barbell rows	3 sets/ 8 reps
Back extensions	3 sets/8 reps

Back extensions by Wendy Upright

Photo by Lisa Brewer

Legs

Squats	3 sets/8 reps
Leg extensions	3 sets /8reps
Leg press	3 sets / 8 reps
Lunges	3 sets /8 reps

 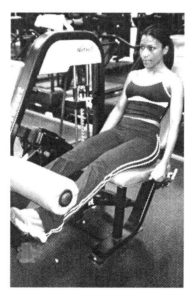

Legs Extensions

Squats

Lunges

Jamneth Cordoba   at work

236

Calves

Standing Toe Raises   3 sets /8reps

Seated toe raises   3 sets / 8 reps

Standing calves raises

Start   **Finish**

Aerobic exercises are done on the same

days or on alternate days. At this point

you can also use a split routine.

Photos by
Frank Marchante

Advance Routine

This routine is for the very advance women; in my opinion only the ones interested in professional bodybuilding need to get to this level.

Monday/Wednesday/ split

Warm-up

Dumbbells swing, stationary bicycles, treadmill walking, ECT.

Chest/ pecs

Bench press	4 sets/8reps
Flying/ peck deck	4 sets/8 reps

Back

Back Extensions	4 sets /8reps
Barbell rows	4 sets /8 reps
Lat pull down to the front	4 sets /8 reps
Lat pull down palms-up	4 sets/8 reps

Shoulders

Dumbbells Lateral raises	4 sets/8reps
Dumbbells Press	4 sets/8 reps
Bend over Dumbbells raises	4sets/8 reps
Dumbbells front raises	4sets/8 reps

Arms

Barbell / Dumbbell Curls	4 sets /8 reps
Triceps Press down	4 sets/8 reps
Preacher curls	4 sets/8 reps

Preacher Curls-Start   *Preacher Curls-Finish*

Tuesday/ Friday

Warm-up

Dumbbells swing, treadmill walking, stationary bicycle

Abdomen

Crunches sit-ups	3 sets /8 reps
Kneeling back kicks	3 sets/8 reps
Side leg kicks	3 sets /8 reps
Leg raise on bench	3 sets /8 rep

Legs/thigh

Squat	4 sets/8 reps
Leg extensions	4 sets /8reps
Leg press	4 sets / 8 reps
Lunges	4 sets /8 reps
Leg curls	4 sets/ 8 reps

Calves

Toe Raises	3 sets /8reps
Seated toe raises	3 sets / 8 reps

Aerobic exercises are done on the same days or even better on alternate days. At this point you can also use a split routine like this one or make one yourself.

Chapter 7

Training Tips

- Try to be regular

- Try to be moderate

- Try to be systematic

- Try to check your progress regularly

- Try to make sure there is plenty of fresh air in the room you are exercising in. Not too cold not to warm.

- Always wear proper clothes and shoes to train

- Do to not over train, but train hard

- Try to always relax, learn to relax

- Try to enjoy dinner. If you are hungry, eat, but eat slowly, eat early, and eat often.

- Sleep well, number of hours depends on individual needs

- Make sure you have at least one bowel movement a day

- Avoid using drugs, medicine

- Keep clean, mentally and morally

- Train, train hard, train hard

Please ask your doctor for a check-up before you follow any advice in this book. It is extremely important to have your doctor approve your exercises.

Fitness

Aerobics is a sustained movement that makes you use oxygen as fuel, like running swimming, etc. Anaerobics is quick, intense exercise like lifting weights, isometrics, etc. Activities that are fast and short help you gain cardiovascular endurance and makes you burn calories such as walking, running, swimming, bicycling. This way you burn glucose and fat as fuel. So keep this in the mind next time you hit the gym. I know many people don't like to do aerobics, but you will continue to burn fat for hours after you stop exercising, even at rest. This is great. Don't you think?
Now you don't have any excuse not to do your cardiovascular exercises, listen to music when using the treadmill or the stationary bicycle, just do it.

There are six types of fitness, including:

Strength   Aerobic Capacity

Agility and balance   Flexibility

Power   Speed

Aerobics Best

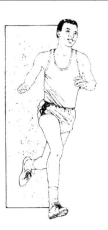

1. Jogging   6. Dancing

2. Cycling   7. Stair Climbing

3. Skip-Rope   8. Walking

4. Tennis   9. Weight-Training

5. Rowing   10. Swimming

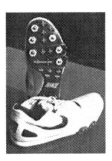

Aerobic Exercises

Laughter is inner jogging.
Norman Cousins

Walking - is probably the simplest and easiest of the aerobics exercises. People walk for many reasons today: for pleasure, to rid themselves of tensions, to find solitude. It can be done inside with a treadmill or outside. It will make you breathe harder and your heart will beat faster, strengthening your Cardiovascular System, burn fat and will tone and conditioned your body. Walking is also a low impact exercise, very good for your knees and feet. Walking is virtually injury-free and has the lowest dropout rate of any form of exercise. Walking can be as good as running or riding a bike. You can do it by yourself or with company. You must keep up the pace. Walk fast for a couple of minutes, go slower for another couple of minutes then fast again. Do it for 30 minutes, three or four times a week. Some benefits of walking are:

- Better cardiovascular fitness
- Decrease body fat
-

- Better lung capacity
- Stronger legs

Treadmill - This equipment is found in every gym. A good walk in this equipment is comparable to a walk or a jog outside. I will recommend walking fast for 2 minutes and then slowing down for another 2 minutes alternating, three to four times a week for about 30 minutes .Better for your knees and back than running or jogging in the pavement. You don't have to worry about weather, traffic or dogs. Excellent.

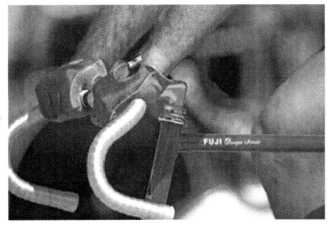

Go out and have some fun

Cycling - Very good for people with back problems. Less stress is placed on your feet and ankles. Great as a conditioning exercise, will build the Quadriceps(front of the thighs) Same here, go fast then slow down, keep this up for about 30 minutes, 3 times a week.

Stair Climbing - Tremendous conditioning exercise. Great for the heart, lunges and losing fat. You will get in shape in no time. Go up and down the stairs, increase time as you get into better shape

Skip Rope - Very good conditioning exercise. Good for lungs, heart, fat loss, it's a legs and calf builder. Alternate from foot to foot and do about 75 jumps per minute. It can be hard to feet and shins if you do it on a hard surface and don't wear appropriate footwear. Jump for 2 or three minutes alternating fast and slow, stop for a minute, repeat again. Four times a week for 15 min.

Running in place - with knees high, also very good cardio exercise. You may raise your feet higher as you get in better shape. Excellent indoor exercise. Three times a week for about 15 min.

Running/Jogging - Probably one of the best known exercises. You must be careful to avoid shin splints and pulled Achilles' tendon. Try to run on the grass, it's less dramatic that running on pavement. Wear good running shoes. The problem with this exercise is the weather, traffic, dogs. You can do it three times a week for about 30 min. Increase the distance or the pace to progress.

Jelena Djordjevic

WNBF 2004 1st place

Ms. Exercise

Figure World

Championship

Photo Lisa Brewer

Stationary Bicycle - Excellent, especially if you are overweight. Adjust the tension to your physical needs. High tension will help you build thigh muscles. Keep tension down for better cardiovascular section. Three to four times a week for 30 min. Go fast slow, slow down, and alternate.

Rowing Machine - A great aerobic exercise. Excellent for arms, back, and legs and at the same time you get your cardiovascular benefit. Four times a week for about 20 min . Great.

Swimming – A very popular and recommended exercise among doctors and therapists. Excellent aerobic exercise keep in mind that some experts think it does not decrease body fat. Well, this you have to find out for yourself. Do it three times a week for 30 min. For safety reasons don't swim alone.

Mini Trampoline - This equipment is becoming popular. The theory behind it is that it's less traumatic to your knees and heels. Try it and see if it works for you. I'm listing it here for information.

Jumping Jacks - Who doesn't remember this exercise in gym classes at school? Jumping jacks has its merits. Better to practice on the grass to make it less traumatic on your heels and knees. Do about 30 reps, increasing reps as you get in shape, four times a week.

Dancing - My favorite, dancing. As a matter of fact, I go dancing every week. I would even go dancing on the nights before most of my major competitions. I believe that because of my dancing I was always in good cardiovascular shape. I dance everything and all night, too.

** British scientists came to the conclusion that treadmills are better for fat burning than stationary bikes and elliptical machines. They claim that a person jogging on a treadmill at about 70 % to 75% of their maximum heart rate burn more fat per hours than in any other machine. There you have it.

The greatest wealth is health. ~Virgil

Warm-up

Let's talk briefly about warm-ups. Your warm-up should not be very long, but on the other hand it should be long enough. The length of a satisfactory warm-up varies from individual to individual and it's different with age. It will help you go from a resting state to prepare you to more demanding exercise. Five to ten minutes of warming up will be enough. In the long run it will prevent you from getting strains, muscle pulls, etc.

After warming-up you can begin stretching. My warm ups consist of a lighter set then I would go up on weight of the same exercise, making my warm-up part of my first sets. I also do some stretching here or there as I go along. I recognize the importance to warm-up and stretching .Although for some individuals it is more important than others. Get to know your body and your needs.

Try it out to find out how much warm-up you need and what works for you. Don't waste too much energy on this, but just enough, so you have plenty of energy for your heavy and intensive workout. Warm ups are good, but keep them short and to the point.

Stretching Exercises

Stretching should be a part of an exercise program. Now it is common to find coaches in all different sports, athletes and dance instructors do stretching exercises. Stretching I believe is very important to weight training, you can do them as a warm–up or you can do them by themselves. Stretching after a warm up prepares muscles for exercise. Stretching after working out will improve flexibility.

Stretch a little beyond your safety zone, but do not push above pain, never stretch a cold muscle and make sure you are in the correct position, never bounce in your stretch, exhale into the stretch, inhale when you release. Stretch at least 3 times a week for 15 min. Stop right away if you feel pain.

1 - Leg lift

Stand erect, lift your leg, and hold it straight in front of you. Hold leg for a count of three. Do both legs 5 times each.

2 - Circles

Standing erect, hold your arms straight out as if you were to fly. Rotate your arms slowly in a circle, backwards then forwards. Do10 in one direction then do 10 more the other way.

3 - Neck Rotation

Standing erect, rotate your head slowly one-way, then the other way. Do 10 reps each way.

4 - Walks

Sitting in a stool or chair, walk your hands between your knees, you should try to place your hands flat on the floor, stretch it a bit, and hold count for 10 seconds. Don't bounce, do 10 reps each time trying to go a little farther. Take your time in accomplishing this, go slowly at first.

5 - Pull up

Bend forward like touching your toes grab each ankle with both hands pull up for a few seconds, release do 10 reps.

6 - Side Bends

Standing straight raise your left arm high and place your other hand against your right leg. Stretch upward as high as you can with your left hand while you bend your body to your right. Alternate left and right. Repeat 10 times.

7 - Calves Stretches

Stand a foot away from a wall. Keep your body straight and lean forward. Keep both heels on the floor until you feel the stretch in your calves. Repeat 5 times.

8 – Thigh Stretches

Lay down on the floor bend your knee and grasp your knee with your hand and hold for 30 seconds. Release and alternate 5 times with both knees.

9 - Triceps Stretches

With arms over head, gently pull one elbow behind the head and with the other hand, hold the stretch for a few seconds and switch arms, repeat 5 times each.

10 - Upper back/Chest stretches

Grasp hands behind back and lift them up until you feel a good stretch. Release and repeat for 5 times.

Stretching is real good for your muscles. There are many good stretching exercises. Stretching must be done after the muscles are warmed never cold. Remember spend most of your time hitting the weights, you are a bodybuilder. Don't over do it be cautious.

Stretching is a must for both men and women

Lisa Brewer WNBF 2003 Ms. Exercise Figure World Championship

Photos Courtesy of www.Lisabrewer.com

Muscle Secret

My routine will not guarantee that you will develop a Mr. Championship body, unless you have great genetics, train hard and dedicate yourself. It will however, help you develop your physical potential to your maximum. If you follow my advice in this book, you will be on your way to a strong, healthy, more attractive looking body. You will look better in your clothes and you will have a better, nicer outlook on life. Exercises do wonders for the mind, body, and soul.

Bodybuilders are always looking for the best and fastest ways to add muscle. Learning the fundamentals of how a muscle works and the range of movements will help you know the basics to have a clear and a better understanding of why and how they work.

According to doctors there are about 261 muscles in the human body and they work together with tendons, 70% is water and 22% is protein. The **real secret** to get huge, massive, strong is progressive resistance, in others words **ADDING WEIGHT**. The time to start bodybuilding is **NOW**. No matter if you are 18 or 55 years old. The secret is, are you ready for this? That **there is no secret**, just hard, hard, and constant workouts, balanced healthy meals, and rest and recuperation. This is the **real secret**.

3× Mr. Olympia- Huge, Ripped and Strong

Japan Posing Exhibition and Seminar

A remarkable photo of the Myth   *Photo Bodybuilding Magazine, Japan*

Another unbelievable photo of Oliva   *Oliva's trade mark pose*

Japan Seminar

Photos Bodybuilding Magazine, Japan

*Photos Bodybuilding
Magazine, Japan*

Sergio and his Fans - Japan

Oliva brought on a commotion wherever he went.

253

Bodybuilding Magazine, Japan

Sergio Oliva a Genetic Phenomenon. One of a kind.

Bodybuilding Magazine, Japan

Sergio Oliva the only man to ever defeat Arnold Schwarzenegger in the Mr. Olympia contest

Beginners Routine

This Program is brief and to the point

3 sets-8 reps ea /3 times a week

Barbell – Machine

Chest

3x8 Bench Press

3x8 Flyes/peck

Barbell–Machine

Back

3x8 Dumbbell Row Motion

3x8 Lat Pulldown to the front

3x8 Chin to the Front

Barbell–Machine

Shoulder

3x8 Lateral Raises

3x8 Presses behind Neck

Barbell–Machine

Arms

3x8 Standing Biceps Barbell Curl

3x8 Lying Triceps Barbell Extension

3x8 Barbell Preacher-Scott Curl

3x8 Press Down on Lat Machine

Barbell–Machine

Legs

3x8 Squats

3x8 Leg Extensions

Calves

3x8   Seated Calf Raises

There you have it, a good beginner's workout, after about 3 or 4 months, you could add one more set to each exercise and one or two more new exercises per body part or muscle. After three or four months, then you are ready to move to the intermediate workout and you can split your routine if necessary. But go slowly at the beginning this is when you are going to make the most progress, so make the most out of it. After six or seven months, you are ready to move to the advance workout. Good luck.

Bend over Lateral Raises

Dumbbell Row Motion

Presses behind Neck

Chin to the Front

Intermediate Routine

Monday & Thursday - Chest, Back, Shoulders

Chest

Bench Press
1 x 50 warm-up
5 x 10
Super Set with Dips
5 x 10

Bent Arms laterals Flyes/Peck Deck
1 x 25 warm-up

Super Set with incline Bench Press
5 x 10

Dips

Shoulders

Bend Forward Dumbell Raises
5 x 20

Super Set with Lateral Raises
5 x 20

Flyes

Back

Rowing

Bar Rowing
1 x 15 warm-up
5 x 10

Super Set with Lat Pull to Neck
1 x 15 warm-up
5 x 10

Press Behind Neck
1 x 15 warm-up
5 x 10

Lat Pull to Neck

Super Set with Decline Dumbell Pullover
5 x 15

Pull Down to Chest on Lat Machine
5 x 10

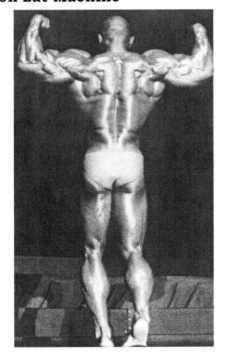

Out of this world!

Tuesday & Friday - Legs, Calves, Abdominals.

Legs

Squats
1 x 50 warm-up
1 x 25
8 x 10

Super Set With Leg Curls
1 x 20 warm-up
1 x 15
8 x 10

Super Set with Standing Calve Raises
5 x 20

Leg Extensions
1 x 15
5 x 10

Super Set With Seated Calve Raises
5 x 20

Abdominals

Crunch Sit-ups
5 x 30

Super Set With Leg Raises
5 x 30

**I like to use a 4 x 4 to keep my heels elevated.

Squats

Leg Curls

Sit-ups

Wednesday & Saturday - Arms

Biceps

Standing Barbell Curl
1 x 25 warm up
5 x 15

Dumbbell curl

Sitting alternating Dumbbell curl
5 x 10

Curl On Scott Curl Machine

5 x 10

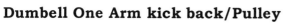

Triceps

Pulley Triceps push down
1 x 35 warm-ups
5 x 10

French Triceps curls
5 x 10 - 15

Dumbell One Arm kick back/Pulley
5 x 10 – 15

Forearms

Reverse Curls
10 x 12

**Scott Curl
Machine**

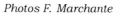

Photos F. Marchante

Advance Routine

The following routine is a six-day routine beginning on Monday and ending on Saturday. Sunday must be a day of complete rest. Your proper weight will be determined according to the affixed number of repetitions, which is eight to ten.

The following warm-up must be done every day before your routine begins!

Sit-ups	3 sets	50 reps
Side Bend Twist with stick	3 sets	60-200 reps
Behind Neck		
Leg Raises	3 sets	20-50 reps
Side Bend twist with stick	3 sets	60-200 reps
Behind Neck		
Seated Calf Raises	5 sets	15 reps
Standing Calf Raises	5 sets	15 reps

Monday and Thursday-all of the following are combination sets!

Bench Press	8 sets	8-10 reps
Wide Grip chins	5 sets	8-15 reps
Pull Down- close grip	3 sets	8-10 reps
Chins behind Neck	3 sets	8-10 reps
Incline Bench Press	3 sets	8-10 reps
Upright Rowing	3 sets	8-10 reps
Seated Press-front	3 sets	8-10reps
Front Lateral Raises	3 sets	8-10 reps
Dumbbell Flyes /Peck-deck	5 sets	8-10 reps
Parallel bar dips	5 sets	8-10 reps

Tuesday and Friday –all of the following are combination sets!

Standing curl	5 sets	8-10 reps
Pull down triceps	5 sets	8-10 reps
Preacher-Scott curl	5 sets	8-10 reps
French curl triceps	5 sets	8-10 reps
Sitting Dumbbell biceps curl	3 sets	8-10 reps
Concentration bicep curl	3 sets	8-10 reps
Triceps Extensions	3 sets	8-10 reps
French triceps Press	3 sets	8-10 reps

Wednesday and Saturday-all of the following are combinations sets!

Sit-ups	10 sets	50 reps
Side Bend twist with stick	10 sets	60-200 reps
Leg Raises	5 sets	20-50 reps
Side Bend with stick	5 sets	60-200 reps
Squats-with weight	5 sets	8-10 reps
Squats no weight/not show	3 sets	25 reps
Leg Extensions	5 sets	8-10 reps
Reversal Leg Curl	5 sets	8-10 reps

Saturday

I do the same exercises as Wednesday plus a few sets for all over the body. It all depends on how I feel that particular day, on my mood, and if I think I need to workout more on a particular area.

I never contract a muscle at the top of the rep, I move it in a continuous tempo in a non-lockout fashion, keeping tension on the muscles all the time and not letting them relax.

I have used different workouts through my life, but I always work triceps and biceps together. I also always work chest and back together. Don't let the magazines fool you, its bullshit! There is no secret only hard work. Try to hit the muscle from all angles, for example, when I do triceps extension with a cable then I do a triceps extension with a barbell. Then I move to a lying French curl with a barbell. As you can see, I have worked the triceps from all angles. Keep in mind that my routine can change depending on the situation. If I'm trying to gain weight, or if a competition is getting closer.

If I'm trying to gain weight I do fewer sets and increase the weight. If a contest is approaching I train lighter and increase the reps because I'm trying to burn. I also never stop working out just because I feel the pump, I move to the next exercise.

Sunday is your day of rest. Make it a good one!

Much Success to you!
Sergio

"NEVER MISTAKE MOTION FOR ACTION"
ERNEST HEMMINGWAY

Get Big-Massive Routine

The best way to build massive size is to work the major muscles while using heavy basic exercises. No way out. Heavy weight will stimulate muscle fiber whereas light weights will not.

Using a high protein diet is as important as doing heavy exercises, pay attention to your diet, sleep and rest. It will help you grow. Growth and repair will happen when you are sleeping and resting.

Take a good vitamin and an Amino Acid supplement and about 1 gram of protein for each pound of body weight. For example 175 lb, 175 grams of protein.

These exercises have not only helped me get massive but most of the bodybuilding champions too. I like to use the pyramid system, adding weight as I go on.

1977 WBBA Paris –   *Photo: Denie*

266

Mass Size Routine

1- Squats - One of my favorite exercises. The king of all exercises develops your thighs as well as also the heart and lungs. Squats will bring growth in people who have a hard time adding size, weight and bulk. Just ask any champion about the result they get from doing squats. Place the weight on the top of your shoulders with feet flat or in a block. Lower into a squat position with the upper body straight, head up. Inhale on the way down, exhale on the way up. Super set with pullovers.

2 - Breathing Pullover - Breathing pullover can be done with dumbbell, barbell or machine. They are done after heavy squats. Do not use much weight here. Lying down on a flat bench using a dumbbell or a barbell at arm's length, bring it back over your head with arms almost straight all the way back, inhaling deep and exhaling when bringing arms up.

Nautilus Machine Pullovers

3 - Bench Press-Lying flat on a flat bench, use a wide grip, holding the barbell at arm's length, lower the bar until it touches your upper  chest. Inhale on the way down exhale on the way up. The best exercise to pack massive upper body.

4 - Incline Barbell Press - Great exercise for upper body and front deltoids thickening. With Barbell at arm' length over face, lower the bar to the chest just under the neck, then push it back to arm's length. Again inhale on the way down, exhale on the way up.

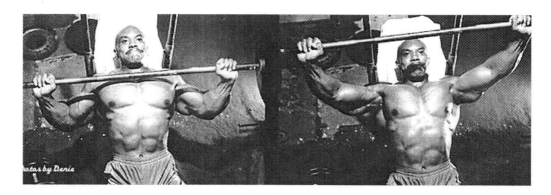

5 - Wide Grip Chins - A great exercise for widening the upper body. Use a wide grip and pull up until your chin is over the bar, lower all the way down to get a good stretch. Chin in front is gentler than to the back of the neck for the shoulder. Many people have a hard time just doing a few chins, that's why is easy to use a lat machine instead. I enjoy this one.

6 - Bent-Over Rowing /Rowing Machine –

Terrific for a massive upper back. Grasp a

barbell with a wide shoulder grip; bend

over with back parallel to floor. Keeping

your back straight pull bar to lower chest or

waist. Feel the stretch as the weight goes

down.

7- Lying Triceps Extension- Excellent for

bulking the upper arms. Lying down on a

flat bench hold a barbell with a close grip

right above your forehead, lower the bar

all the way bellow your head, keeping the elbows pointing toward the

ceiling. Bring barbell back up. Repeat.

8 - Dead Lifts - I don't see many people

doing these exercises on the gym anymore.

The dead lift is the most important exercise

for the lower back. Bend legs, bend body

forward, grasp the bar with one palm facing

up and the other palm facing down, bring

body straight up, exhale on the way up

inhale on the way down.

9 - Calf Raises - With body straight and barbell or machine pads over shoulders, heels over block, go up on your toes as far as you can and then down getting a good stretch as you lower the heels toward the floor.

This routine will build **huge size, power** and will make you **big.** Use the heaviest weight you can handle, try to increase 5 pounds each week while using **good form**. This is important to keep training injuries away. Always warm up and cool down. If you are not making progress, then you are probably either not training hard enough or not resting adequate time, not getting the specialized nutrition your body needs or you are training too much. Train hard, rest sufficient, get the nutrition your body needs and you will be impressed and amazed at your growth.

Denie

Huge!

Myth's Tips

There should always be some kind of strength exercises. As a matter of fact, I went to Miami, Florida in Nov 2003 and I explained in my workshop the importance of always including these types of exercises: the squat, clean and jerk, dead lifts, or the snatch.

The Snatch

You lift the weight over your head from the floor in a single move. The bar is pulled upward as high and fast as possible at the same time you move one of your feet aft. Then you regain your upright position. The snatch lifts place a tremendous and different stress on your body.

Dead Lift

Stand close to the heavy bar, bend your knees slightly, keeping the back flat and arms straight, one hand is placed over the bar and the other under the bar, lift the bar up until you are standing straight.
I believe this exercise and the squats are the best strength-muscle building of all.

The Squat

Strengthens the thigh muscle and also has a big effect on the whole body, respiratory system, heart and lunges. I really believe it is impossible to really gain bulk, muscle weight without squats.
All major champions I know have put on pound after pounds onto their bodies doing squats.
With a heavy loaded barbell behind and across your shoulder, keeping the back flat all of the time, squat fully down all the way down.
I like to use a block under my heels, as soon as your buttock touches your heels rise in a slow controlled manner. Reps/sets according to your individual strength and goals, but 3 sets of 12 to 15 reps are ok.

Myth's Tips (Secrets)

1. **Dead lifts** - Always do the dead lift. Today not too many people do it any more.

2. **Squats** - All the way to the bottom. Bottoms touching heels.

3. **Front squats** - Hold barbell in front of chest. Very important for front thighs development.

4. **Parallel dips** - Adding weight, as you get stronger. I have always used it for many reps.

5. **Chin-up** - To the front and behind neck. I use to do many, many reps.

6. **Press and clean -** If you want to become strong and develop a strong back.

7. **Bench press** - Never locking elbows.

These exercises were used by all old timer champions. Today most people do not use them. Do them even if you don't do anything else and watch your body weight and muscle grow, become thicker and become stronger.
These exercises with adequate rest and eating will make a difference like you won't believe. Try it now, do it. See for yourself. I always use them in my routine one way or another.

Notes taken from Sergio Oliva Seminar Saturday, November 29th, 2003 South Florida Bodybuilding, Fitness & Figure Championships.

TRAIN OF THOUGHT

Professional Competition Thoughts

If you want to be as **massive** as you can or be a **bodybuilding champion** you must handle heavy weights and do many reps. I certainly do many, many, heavy reps. Sometimes doing as much as 20-25 sets of six to eight reps. Using heavy weight with intensity is a must to make you massive and strong. Do **basic exercises** like Bench Press, Row Motion, Press, Squat, Barbell curls, etc. Always use the heaviest weight you can handle for 8 to 12 reps. Once in a while **shock** your muscle, change and do light weight and again high reps. Never let your muscles get use to it, keep them guessing, surprising them and you will never stop making gains.

Holding your breath could be dangerous, especially struggling doing the last few heavy reps, it will elevate blood pressure. Breathe in and out at a rhythm every rep and try not to hold it. Keep this in mind when training heavy.

Calories- Remember No more than 20% of your daily calories should come from the good fat; about 50 % or 60% of daily calories should come from complex carbohydrates – fruits – vegetables - whole grain.

Fat- Keep in mind Not all fat is bad, fat as monounsaturated fats in nut, olive oil and omega - 3 fatty acids found in fish, flaxseeds are good for the heart.

Low carbohydrates - My opinion is never to mix carbohydrates with **fats.** Be careful with **sugar** from fruits when getting ready for a competition. Learn which ones to eat and when. Low carbs means low muscle glycogen. This means you will have a hard time keeping your energy up for your daily training. Cut carbohydrates about eight or nine weeks before the contest and do it gradually, the last week do not take any fats & carbs. You should eat some before contest time. How much? Well here you have to learn by experimenting. You are unique, so find out what works for you. One more thing, always **eat your carbs** after your workouts.
I personally never did this for more than a couple of weeks.
Try also eating five to six times a day instead of three big meals. Never eat late in the evenings and make sure to drink plenty of water.

Meat - The leanest cuts of red meat are Sirloin or Top Round. Remove visible fat, grilled is much better.

Poultry - Eat ground poultry and remove the skin from chicken & turkey. This is where most of the fat is found.

Goals – Your goals must be realistic. Make short and long terms goals. Make sure they're achievable. Very important

Cardio Session - In my opinion cardio sessions should always be done after **hitting the weights** or better on alternate days from the weights. Training with weight should be your **priority**, when you have lots of energy unless you are trying to lose **(fat)**. In my opinion moderate to low intensity cardio will make you use glycogen and help you **burn fat.**

Surprise and **shock** your body, do different exercises. Don't let your body get use to your training, so you don't progress anymore, change or adjust your routine.

 Free weights - In my opinion is superior and more effective than any kind of machine. If you are working hard to bring out a **lagging part**, I recommend you start your training routine with a particular muscle to bring out all your energy and enthusiasm into the training session.

Vascularity - Want that **muscularity** look that you see in the champions? Then you must drop your body fat about 7% so you don't have fat covering your muscles. This takes hard work, commitment, discipline and sacrifices, easier said than done right. Control your fluid intake for a competition. This way you achieve a more muscularity look. Watch your sodium intake. Sodium is always hiding in many different ways. Some bodybuilders don't drink water before a contest, they gargle with water or suck on ice, here again you have to find out what works for you.

Building **calves** for many people is a long, hard and extremely difficult task. Not for me. You must focus on them; it may take a long time for some people to develop them. Use full range of motion, feel each rep. Concentrate, work hard, work heavy, make them burn, make your muscle cry out for mercy.

Steroids - Most people know there have been studies that show that steroids make you gain strength, build muscle and lose fat, this is true. Adding weight training will make it more effective, of course. Improvement in performance has also been reported in athletic events. By now I'm sure you know about baseball, football, track & field runners and steroids. However, side effects are very, very dangerous. If you are going to use them regardless of their cons, stick to low dosages. Be careful with those sold in the **black market.** Ask your doctor to check your blood and urine every 4 to 6 weeks. Be careful. Think it over before you do it.

Sun - Make sure to get some **sun,** but not too much. In a previous chapter I mentioned how important sunbathing is for competition.
Keep your mind in something else beside the competition and try to **relax**.

Plateaus - Get to know yourself. Recognize when it's time to change your routine, eating habits, protein intake and carbohydrates. Try new exercises, new routines, take a few days off, change your grip width, reduce the weight, do more reps, change your tempo, frequency, intensity, in other words, keep changing but only when you hit a plateaus, no sense on changing as long as you're making gains. If you follow my advice here, you will always be improving.

Stage presence - Incredibly important, you **must win** the audience, make them **move**, **stand**, **clap**, and **yell**. Give them something special with your posing routine. Make them want more of you, when you leave the posing platform, leave them yelling for more. Practice your **posing** routine many, many times. Make sure to choose **music** that brings people up, with a good beat, it must also match your personality.

The Mighty Back of Sergio Oliva!

Music and the Bodybuilder

It's been known that melody and tempo in music have
an incredible impact on the human body especially in the
heart, circulatory system and your stomach.

Sit down and lift up your feet, listen to some nice music
rhythm. A good music tone relaxes your spirit and even takes you back in time.
You bet it does!

The calming effect of music does wonders for your body; it even brings
down your blood pressure a few points. Fast high beat tempos, can also help
you in your workouts, by giving you an edge somehow.

Some athletes use earphones in the gym when they are working out, to
keep outside noises to a minimum. Others use it so nobody talks to them when
working out and interfere with their workout. Concentrating only on the
exercises and keeping the fire of the spirit going through the workout.

Don't under estimate music. I have always used music one way or
another. I use to go dancing a lot and still do. Give it a try. See what happens.

Youngsters and Bodybuilding

One of the most FAQ'S I get from time to time is if young kids should workout or exercise at an early age.

Let's keep in mind that active growth starts at birth and continues until about age 20 or a little more. My personal thinking is that no one should train with weights or machines at least until they are 16 if they have develop well. If they haven't, then they should wait until they are a little older.

However, kids should exercise before 16. They should play baseball, basketball, soccer, tennis, swim and ride bicycle. Any of these are excellent for a youngster. They can do push-ups, pull-ups, sit-ups and cardio exercises. They can also do stretching exercises, without overdoing it.

Sport is a preserver of health.
~Hippocrates

Now a day lots of kids are fat or obese because most of them spend too much time watching TV, up to 24 hours a week, about 52 days a year or playing computer games. Some live in apartments and don't get to go out and play much. Parents should make time and effort to take their kids to the park to skate, ride a bicycle, or get them involved in a team, it doesn't matter which. This will help keep kids away from drugs, alcohol and keep their mind occupied.

Parents should also try to teach kids to eat a well balanced diet. Not an easy task with so many commercial of fast food restaurants over the TV, 1/3 of all children eat every day in a fast food restaurant, French fries, soft drinks have all been super sized. Hamburgers are at least 22% larger. According to the USDA more than 60% of children are not getting enough calcium. The USDA recommends for youngsters 1,300 milligrams of calcium daily.

Try to at least teach your child to stay away from junk food as much as possible. For example instead of a soda have an orange juice, instead of a hot dog have a turkey sandwich, instead of french fries have some fruit. You only need to make some minor adjustments. When going to visit a place in the second or third floor, don't take the elevator take the stairs instead and have some fun together. Cardio exercises are for everybody in the family.

In today's physical education you don't get that much exercise, many kids stand around waiting, wasting time or refusing to participate.
More than 70% of schools have some kind of vending machine for sodas, candy, etc.

Teach them to drink milk, fruit, and vegetables, spend sometime outdoors breathing natural air and getting some vitamin D from the sun.

Parents can really influence their kid's behavior and health habits, like not smoking or drinking at least in front of them.

This is the way I feel about youngsters and exercising, have fun.

What can parents do?

Often parents don't have time to prepare any kind of dinner. They just head to the nearest take out place.

It is important for parents to have the refrigerator stocked with a variety of healthy foods for our kids to choose from. Make sure your kids are getting a well balanced diet with grains, fruits, vegetables and lean proteins. Emphasize wholesome, low fat choices.

Think of joining your local YMCA or other fitness facility that offer programs for the youngest of the family. Play games, jump rope, skate, jog, play tennis, swim, take a walk together. Limit television and video games and have activities ready where all can participate.

Traveling Exercises

When we are traveling or are away from home there is no excuse not to exercise, this is also the time we tend to over eat, watch it. If you want to take a few days off, go ahead do it. But if you feel like exercising or have to because of a competition or other responsibility I'm including a free hand workout that will help keep you in shape.

You can do 3 sets of 8 reps for each exercise, or even better, 6 sets of 8 reps each depending on your physical strength and stamina.

Warm-up

Body Stretch

Stand with your feet apart and reach high extending your hands all the way up and at the same time standing in your tiptoes do it 8 or 10 times feeling your body stretching. Start slowly and go through these freehand exercises to get your blood moving. Always warm up, don't rush, have a good time. This is what exercising is all about. Enjoy it.

Toe Touch

Reach down keeping your legs a little bent so you won't hurt your back and try to touch your toes with your fingers. Go slow don't bounce. Many years ago this exercise use to be done with straight legs, not anymore.

Thighs

Lunges

From an upright position step out and bend down with the back leg until it barely touches the floor, in smooth rhythm return to the original position, then do the same with the other leg. Great.

The Squat

Probably the best exercise. Everybody knows I like to squat. Stand with your feet apart and place your heels in a block of wood or book, keep your back straight and your head looking straight ahead go down until your body is all the way down, go up and down until you reach the amount of reps you are planning to do, excellent, even without weights.

279

Chest – Shoulders – Triceps

Push-Up

Lie on your stomach. Lift your body pushing with your hands until your arms are locked; now go down slowly until your chest touches the floor. You can place your heels in a chair; hands open wide, hands in a narrow position, to make the exercise harder.

Abdomen

1/4 Sit-Up

Begin with your feet held in place like under a bed and your knees slightly bent. Clasp your hand behind your neck and start raising your upper body but only 1/4 of the way up (exhale as you go up) go down and without resting go up again.

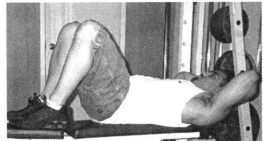 

Knees to Chest

Standing up, lift your knee up until you can clasp it with both hands, pull your knee in and exhale, lower your knee and lift the other one in a rhythmic way without stopping. Very good.

Calves

Calf raise

Take a chair or a table and a piece of wood 2x4 or even a thick book. Place your toes on top of the block or book, hold the back of a chair or a table for balance, lift yourself as far up on the toes as you can, lower yourself until you stretch your heels and touch the floor, keep going up and down without stopping and use no help from your hands, feel the burn and pain in your calves. Nice.

Cardio

If you need to do cardio, running in place or running up and down the stairs for 15 to 20 minutes is an excellent cardiovascular exercise.

There you have it, an excellent freehand exercise routine for traveling days, no excuses now.

Wayne Gallash

Sergio with Lynde Johnson Ms. Olympus-Paris, Nov6, 1977

Chest Expanders/Springs

Chest expanders or springs like most people call them are light and easy to take along on a vacation or when you are away from home. There are many different kinds of chest expanders. Some are made of springs, rubber, or other kinds of materials.

Expanders are good for toning and to gain strength and muscles. You can increase the resistance by adding a spring or two. However the increase from one to two is sometimes a big increase for some people.

The legendary Steve Reeves claimed in his last book Dynamic Muscle Building on page 144 that he used springs and did some workouts with them a few days before his Mr. Universe wining in London.
Here is a list of the best.

1 CHEST PULL-CHEST

Hold the springs in front of you at arms length. Pull the springs outward until it touches the chest while keeping arms straight. Release slowly. Do 2 sets 15 reps ea.

2 OVERHEAD PULL-LATS-CHEST

Hold springs at arms above head, palms facing outward. Pull springs across chest or behind neck (alternate). Release springs back slowly. Do 2 sets 15 reps ea.

3 LATERAL RAISES TO THE FRONT

Hold springs in front of legs, knuckles out. Raise the arms outward sideways. Do 2 sets 15 reps ea.

4 LATERAL RAISES –BACK-DELTOIDS

Springs held across back, knuckles out, raise the arms outward sideways. Do 2 sets 15 reps ea.

CHEST EXPANDERS (CONT)

5 BEND CHEST PULL –CHEST

Bend forward so body is about right angle. Stretch springs out across chest. Release slowly. Do 2 sets 15 reps ea.

6 CURL BICEPS

Hold springs to one side of body with a foot in one handle, with the other hand curl by flexing the arm, contract the muscle at the top of the moment. Release slowly. Do 2 sets 15 reps ea.

7 BOW ARROW-ARMS

One arm straight on line with shoulder level and the other bent in front of chest. Slowly draw out the bent arm to extend it, like aiming a bow & arrow. Do 2 sets 15 reps ea.

8 DIAGONAL CHEST PULL-ARM

One hand holds the springs straight above the head, other hand is holding with arm bend the spring in front of chest. Press bent arm straight to side. Do 2 sets 15 reps ea.

9 LEG PRESS-LEGS

One foot on spring handle, leg bend at chest high, hold the other handle at chest high, pull down foot to floor, extends leg. Do 2 sets 15 reps ea.

10 PUSH FORWARD BACK-CHEST-ARM

Pass spring around the low back, push out spring with both hands to the front. Do 2 sets 15 reps ea.

Free Exercises

Most free exercises are good for your health, keeping you trim, muscular and tone. Keep in mind that these exercises do not give you size-bulk increases .If you are after muscle size you need a resistance work-out no way around it. The only disadvantage of exercises like this is increases in bulk and strength are very limited.
These are the ones I have used one time or another. You can do them when you are on vacation, away from home or just when you are taking some time off from your regular weight workouts or even as a warm up.

1 - ALTERNATE KNEE RAISES

Cardiovascular/Abdomen

Raise knee high to your chest, grasp knee with your hands, and pull knee to chest.
Do two sets of 15 with ea leg.

2- Knees Raises

Abdomen

Seat on a bench, raise knees to chest; hold them for a few seconds, lower knees slowly under control, breathe out when raising knees, breathe in when lowering. Never hold your breath. Do two sets of 15 reps.

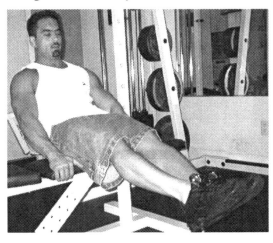
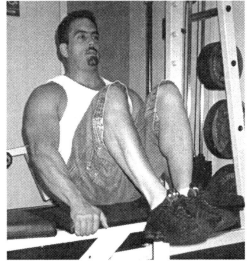

3- PUSH-UPS
Chest-Deltoids-Triceps
Lower your body until chest touches the floor, keeping body straight. Rise again in a rhythmic way. Do two sets of 15 reps, later as you get stronger raise your feet support higher, to give you some kind of resistance or make it harder.

Photo by Denie

4-Door Pull-up (no shown)
Lats/Legs
Standing in front of a door, grasp the doorknob, bend your knees and go down until arms are fully extended. Pull up to the starting position trying to use your arms only. Repeat.

5-Chin-ups
Back-Arms
You can do this exercise in the park using for a chinning bar one of those kids swing sets or even a tree, or you can buy a portable one. Grasp the bar with palm facing you, pull yourself up until your chin touches the bar, lower and repeat without stopping or your feet touching the floor.

6- **Jumping Jacks**
Cardiovascular

Make sure to lift your feet high as you possibly can. Jump light on your toes for 3 or 4 minutes. Do two sets of 10min. As you progress add more time.

The Myth doing Jumping Jacks

7 - **TOE TOUCHES**
Abdomen
Try to touch your toes, with arms stretched and knees lightly bent, bend over and touch your toes. Do two sets of 15 reps.

Photo by Denie

8 – **1/4 SITS –UP**
Abdomen
Lying down on floor, knees bent. Raise just your shoulders and head, breathe out, contract your abdominal muscle, breathe in and lower your shoulder to floor. Do it without stopping two sets 15 reps each.

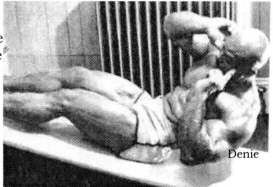

Denie

9- **Body twists**
Abdomen/Oblique
Use a broomstick; place it behind your neck, arms stretched along broomstick. Twist left to right.
Do two sets of 15 to each side.

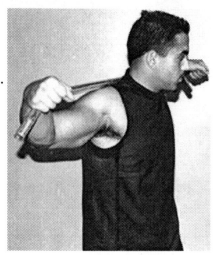

10 - **The Squat**
Thigh Muscles

Probably the best exercise. Everybody knows I like to squat. Stand with your feet apart and place your heels in a block of wood or book, keep your back straight and your head looking straight ahead go down until your body is all the way down, go up and down until you reach the amount of reps you are planning to do, excellent, even without weight.

11 – **Chair/Bar dips**
Triceps

Place hands on bars or on the back edge of a chair.
Bend arms slowly, lower body, push back up using arms.

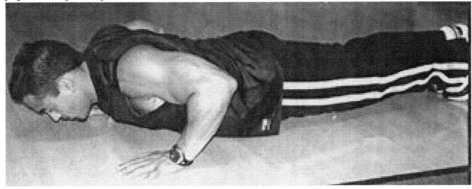

12 - **Triceps Push-ups**
Triceps

Assume a regular push- up position but with hands close together,   fingers touching each other forming a triangle. Lower chest as much as possible   and slowly push up. Repeat 15 times.

Frank Marchante Jr.
Doing Push-ups

Photos F. Marchante

Photo Robert Kennedy

Chapter 8

Seminar with Sergio

This list was compiled from the many seminars I have held worldwide and these are some of the questions the fans have asked me in the seminars.

1. What do you recommend for a beginner to gain size and weight?

Work out the big muscles, chest, back, legs. Use heavy weights, if you can do more than 8 or 10 reps, use more weight. Eat all you can, but make it good healthy meals, no junk food. Don't over train.

2. Do you believe in taking extra protein?

If you are working hard, use it. Any supplement that has amino acids is good.

3. How much weight did you use when doing squats?

Between 650 and 770 pounds.

4. How much do you weigh right now?

Now I weigh around 225 pounds and I'm 5' 10".

5. What do you do for your shoulders?

Presses behind the neck and to the front, lateral raises to the front and back.

6. What do you do for your arms?

Standing barbell curl, dumbbell curl, Preacher curl, barbell triceps extension, pulley triceps extension, and dips.

7. What about for forearms?

Reverse curl and forearms roller, 10 to 12 reps per set.

8. What kind of diets did you go on for a major competition?

The most I stayed on a diet was for 2 or 3 weeks. I couldn't go more than that. Between contests I ate anything, rice, beans, chocolate shake, coca cola, pizza. I tried to balance my meals. I didn't eat junk food everyday. Although, my kids sometimes talked me into going to fast food restaurants, like Burger King, I like it too.

9. Did you ever use PHA (peripheral heart action) system?

No, never.

10. Did you use the split system?

Yes, but in my own way.

11. Do you take time off from training?

Never, I like to train year round.

12. What is the time you like to train?

From 4 pm to 7 pm.

13. Do you change your training workouts?

Never, I do the same year after year. It works for me, why change?

14. What do you prefer, machine over barbell and dumbbells?

99% of all champions were made with barbells and dumbbells, but of course machines help too. Some exercises are better in the machines than others are, it depends.

15. There is a controversy about squats. Did you do them? Do you still do them?

I use to do squats all the time. I don't any more because of a job related accident. I hurt my knees and later they found a cyst and I had it removed.

16. You used full or ½ squats?

Full squat to the front and to the back, all the way down.

17. How many hours do you sleep? Do you take muscle naps?

4 or 5 hours every day. Naps never.

18. Do you workout with a cold and flu?

I have never caught a cold; believe it or not this is true. When my
kids get a cold they always complain by saying why me? How come you never get
a cold?

19. Did you ever get high blood pressure from lifting heavy

weights?

Never.

20. Do you workout with pain? Do you workout when you have

an injury?

Never got one from training.

21. Did you take extra protein?

Sometimes I use to. I took Blair protein; I also made milk shakes with protein
powder, and bananas.

22. Did you use to take B-12 vitamins?

Yes I did, one shot a month.

23. What about vitamin C?

I use to take 200 milligrams a day.

24. Can you tell me your muscularity preparation for a contest?

I use to run on the treadmill, swim, eat healthy foods and do extremely hard
workouts.

25. Did you ever take steroids? Which ones?

Yes, but only after my first Mr. Olympia and if I took it was because the other
competitors were doing it. I took one tablet of Dianabol a day for two or three
weeks and one shot a month of Deca or Winstrol.

26. Did you run? Do you think it's good?

Yes I ran, once or twice a week, and I think it's excellent.

27. Any secrets or anything special for a contest?

There are no secrets only hard workouts, good healthy meals and a lot of dancing.

28. Greatest influence in bodybuilding?

John Grimek and Steve Reeves.

29. How important is genetics in bodybuilding?

The truth is that it's very important for a bodybuilder in order to be a champion.

30. What do you think of modern drugs? Creatine? DHEA? Insulin?

Chromium Picolinate?

It's crazy, what people are taking now. I don't think it's good to manipulate the body like that. What happened to diets, rest, and exercise? I don't mean to say there are no good products in the market, there are.

31. What is the perfect workout schedule for you?

Between 4 pm and 7:30 pm, two hours before dinner or two hours after dinner.

32. Do you like to train with a training partner or alone?

I prefer to train with a partner but a partner has to train with similar weights and use similar equipment to be productive.

33. Your philosophy of life?

Be free, support my family and self, be a good father and man as I humanly can. Have fun, look for hard workouts and of course worship God.

34. What is a typical day for Sergio Oliva?

Nothing special, breakfast, lunch, work, the gym, and dinner. I also spend some quality time with my son and daughter.

35. Do you use negatives reps?

Never bothered.

36. What about cheat reps?

A little here and there, not much.

37. Did you use forced reps?

Never got into it.

38. Did you ever use peak contraction?

I never did that.

39. Rest and pause? Have you used it?

Never used it, no.

40. Do you do strict reps?

Yes I try to do strict reps.

41. Do you do Super sets?

I do, for example bench press with chin; I combine exercises one after the other. You may say I do it my own way.

42. What do you do for biceps?

I do heavy standing curls, preacher curls, seated dumbbell curls and concentration curls.

43. What about pyramid reps?

This is the one I like to use; I'll go up in weight as I go down on reps.

44. What is your speed training?

I use a medium tempo, not to slow not to fast..

45. Do you use a lifting belt?

I use one most of the time.

46. Do you exercise at random or do you have a routine?

Most of the time I use my routine, and some days I do what comes naturally, you can call it instinctive.

47. Which one is your favorite part?

No favorite part.

48. Which one is your favorite exercise?

None, but if I had to pick one I'd say clean & jerk or the squat..

49. How do you warm-up?

Using the pyramid system, I start with 180 pounds and go up as I train.

50. Do you eat meat?

Yes, I'm a steak lover, I love beef.

51. Do you diet for a long time?

No, never.

52. How important is exercise form for you?

It is important somehow, I'm not a slave of it.

53. Do you think that exercising one limb at a time is better?

It depends on the exercise or that particular day.

54. Do you keep a training diary?

Not really, but I have started to and then let go.

55. Can you tell me your involvement with Arthur Jones?

What a true gentleman he is, very intelligent man, I went to Florida to train with him and the first thing he did was to measure my arms cold just getting off the plane, and mine was the only one over 20 inches COLD, no matter what the magazines say. It was a privilege to have known this man.

56. Were your forearms so big at one time that you couldn't flex your biceps?

True, my forearm was a little over 20 inches.

57. What was your waist size during your best shape?

27 inches.

58. Is it true that your head was smaller than your arms?

Yes it's true, one time they were. Arthur Jones measured them and found out my waist was also smaller than my legs.

59. Which sport do you like?

Boxing, baseball, football, and bodybuilding of course.

60. Would you like your son to follow your foot steps in bodybuilding?

As a matter of fact, he's already competing.

61. Would you help him?

Of course I would, I would help him in anything he decides.

62. Have you seen Ali, Forman, and Frazier's daughters? What do you think?

Yes I have, but I wouldn't want my daughter to box or do bodybuilding.

63. Do you have any idea of where bodybuilding is headed in the future?

For sure we have to push for fair competitions. Contests should not be a one-man property.

64. Would you compete in the future for the Master Mr. Olympia?

No way, to see an old champion half his best so people will remember him old and out of shape, no that's not for me.

65. Did you take any laxative to lose water before a competition?

I never did that.

66. Did you get a suntan before a competition?

Yes I did.

67. Did you ever get nervous before coming out on stage during a competition?

Not really, as a matter of fact I liked it. I liked to make contact with the fans.

68. What was your gym's name?

Power and Beauty.

69. Do you drink anything before working out?

Nothing, just plain water.

70. How many hours after eating do you workout?

I eat two hours after a workout. I never eat for two hours before training.

71. What did you use to do the night before a competition?

Sometimes I went dancing, other times I stayed home and watched a movie. It all depended on that particular competition, but I did nothing different.

72. What year did you get divorce?

In 1987 and I have a son and a daughter with my ex- wife.

73. What do your daughter and son think of you? Do they understand that you are the best bodybuilder in the world?

They understand. My son's friends come by and look at the pictures all the time and when we go out and people want my picture or autograph or just say hello, they know and accept it.

74. Did Larry Scott and Chuck Sipes use to train in Duncan's gym in Chicago where you used to train?

Not true.

75. Did Bob Cajda teach you?

No, he just helped me with some poses. He is a friend but I haven't seen him in a while.

76. With what score did you pass your police test?

With over 70 points.

77. How old were you when you started bodybuilding?

About 22 that's a little too old, you should begin around age 17.

78. Sergio did women chase you?

To be honest, yes, I was young, built and a very good dancer, the answer is all the time.

79. According to the experts, you are the greatest bodybuilder that has ever lived. How does that feel?

I don't think I'm the best, I love the sport, I like competing, but it feels good to be recognized as one of the best in the sport. It never went to my head.

80. What kind of chin-up do you like to do?

To the front and to the back.

81. What is your waist now?

30 inches.

82. Did you ever have pants made especially for you?

All the time, I had to!

83. Did you ever get flexibility problems as a result of weight training?

No never, I was and still am very flexible.

84. Do you think you ever reached your maximum potential?

Yes I did, I think it was for the Mr. Olympia in Germany in 1972 and a couple of other times.

85. Do you stop working out when you get the pump?

No, you just finish a heavy curl and get a pump; you go then and do some preacher curls and others exercises to keep the pump going.

86. What was your secret for definition?

I ran in the treadmill for one hour and some days I swam.

87. I heard you had many operations, how many and why?

I've had 17 operations, 5 were major, and 12 arthroscopy on my shoulders and knees. I got hurt in my job, never working out.

88. What do you take after the prejudging? Any secrets?

Just juice, that's all, juice.

89. What did you use to do after a major competition?

Go eat pizza and go dancing all night long.

90. How long did you have your gym?

I had it for 10 years.

91. What exercise do you do first?

Bench, always bench.

92. Why did you stop competing?

In 1997 I was foot patrolling and I fell down in the snow doing my police work and I hurt my knees, fractured my elbow and needed to get operated. Both of my knees ended up being replaced. I can't do squats no more. Nothing substitutes squats for mass for competition. Now I just maintain my legs. That's when I called it "quits" for competition.

93. There is a rumor that you benched-pressed 400 pounds, 50 reps without stopping. Is it true?

This rumor is true I did it without stopping.

94. Did you ever do Olympic lifting?

Yes back in Cuba. I use to compete in 181 lb and for a while I was competing with the A.A.U. I was competing in Olympic lifting and physique contest at the same time.

95. Who gave you the name The Myth?

Rick Wayne tried to get the Glory, but nobody really knows.

96. Who is you favorite bodybuilding champion?

John Grimek and Steve Reeves.

97. What was your maximum bench press?

The most I did was 530 pounds, but I could do 50 reps with 400 pounds. Remember, I was a bodybuilder not a weightlifter.

98. What do you do to keep that small waist of yours? Any secrets?

This is my structure, but I do sit ups, leg raises and twists with a Stick. My waist responds immediately to sit-ups and leg raises. I only do 3 or 4 sets of each, not too much.

99. You have given seminars all over the world. Can you tell me where the most enthusiasm is?

There's a lot of enthusiasm all over the world, it is hard to say, Germany, USA, many places.

100. What kind of chin-ups do you do?

I do wide grips on a v –bar, I do front, behind the neck and also with a very wide grip. I do lots and lot of reps.

101. What do you do for your thighs?

Squat all the way down, thigh extensions for the front and leg curl for the leg biceps, sometimes leg presses and hacks squat.

102. How do you know you have reached a sticking point?

When the weight you're using can't go beyond for a couple of weeks.

103. How many sets do you do?

I do lots of sets. Some exercises I do 5 sets, others I do 3 sets, sometimes I have done over 15 sets. Most of the time, I do a lot of different exercises but usually 3 or 4 sets of each.

104. Sergio they say you are flamboyant, is it true? Why?

Probably they say that because of the car I drive or maybe it's because of the medallion I wear around my neck or maybe because of the clothes I wear.

105. Do you drink?

Once in a while in a party, or when I go out and have a great time.

106. Do you smoke?

Never, I don't and never will.

106. Would you change anything in your life?

Nothing.

107. When did you retire from the police force?

I retired in 2003.

108. What are you doing now that you are retired?

I'm also judging bodybuilding competitions and speaking at seminars. I would also like to help young kids stay away from drugs by helping them train at the YMCA.

109. Do you plan to stay in Chicago always?

Yes, Chicago is my home. My kids were born here and I guess I'll die here too.

110. Did you ever count calories or fat grams?

Never.

111. Do you limit some foods from your diet?

No, never.

112. Do you keep an eye on food portions

Not really, only sometimes when I was getting ready for a competition but hardly ever.

113. Do your son Sergio Jr. is going to follow your steps in bodybuilding?

He is competing right now; he has won a couple of competition.

114. How long are you planning to work out?

Until God allows me to.

Sergio's Seminar always interesting, controversial and fun

Guest speaker

Sergio's Seminars are informative, fun and pack

Signing autographs

Chatting with fans

Chicago 2001

At a hotel in Chicago

Sergio and Author – Frank Marchante at a gym in Chicago

Miami 2004

With Fitness Trainer Frank Marchante Jr.

Sergio's Semiar with Frank Marchante and Frank Jr. (Florida)

Like Father Like Son

Most muscular pose- Awesome !

Sergio Oliva Jr. 2006

WABBA & WBBG

Oliva's physical perfection combined with rugged muscularity

With W.B.B.G. president Dan Lurie

1977 WABBA Paris, Bill Grant (USA) left, Sergio, Tony Emmott (England)

WABBA–Paris 1977

Paul Wynter, Tony Emmontt, Sergio and Bill Grant

The legendary Steve Reeves congratulates Sergio at the 1977 WABBA in Paris.
Left is Tony Emmott (England) right is Bill Grant (USA)

307

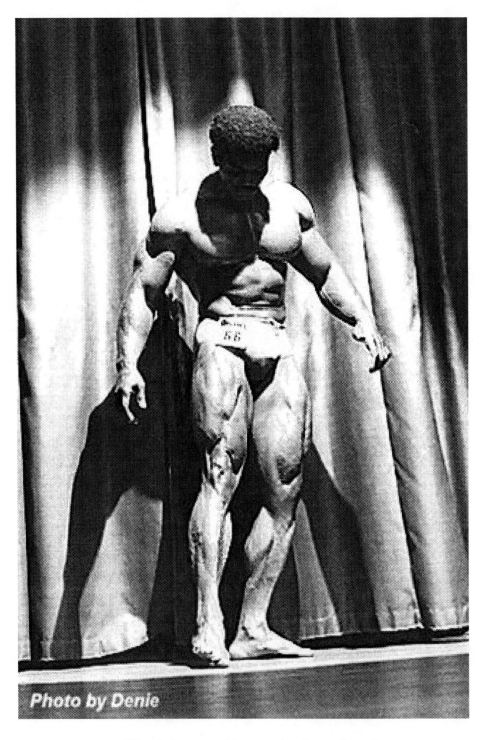

Oliva is huge and impressive from all angles

Judging at the WBBG Mr. America 1973, Eddie Silvestre, Don Peters and Sergio

Sergio Oliva congratulating Chris Dickerson at the1973 WBBG Mr. America

Prejudging break photo, top row judges: Eddie Silvestre, Don Peters, Sergio, Mr America Jim Morris, promoter Bob, WBBG president Dan Lurie, next man over Mr. America and Mr. Universe Reg Lewis

J U D G E   D A Y

Photos: Art Zeller

Amazing! Check the cut on Sergio's thigh

310

Photo Robert Kennedy

Champion Talk

A while back a journalist questioned me about other champs and here's what I said.

Arnold

Symmetry ok, good arms, no forearms, big waist, a regular chest, good back, small cut legs, really bad calves. In my opinion his physique was not perfect.

Chuck Sipes

A good friend of mine for many years, big pectorals, rare, different, very, very good guy.

Lou Ferrigno - The Hulk

He had bad luck, good guy, great athlete, maybe because he is so tall he never got the physique he desired, extremely good symmetry, terrible calves, a big waist, regular chest, and small forearms, more or less like Arnold's body.

Franco Columbu

Too short, strong like a bear, but for me, not a Mr. Olympia body.

Frank Zane

A very good friend, a very lovely wife, both good friends, very symmetrical body. Could he have won the Mr. Olympia if we had been competing (the big guys)?

John Grimek

Perfection, strong like a bull, I always admired him, a perfect body, he used to pose like an eagle. Super strong in the press and others lifts.

Steve Reeves

Perfect, a beautiful physique, not like John Grimek that had beauty and power.

Reg Park

Same body as Arnold, no forearms, no calves, big waist.

Rick Wayne

A very good body, not for international competition, but had a great body.

Casey Viator

Perfect, strong, something like John Grimek, strong like a bear.

Bill Pearl

Good for national competition, but not for Mr. Olympia competition.

Larry Scott

Good athlete, good forearms, good biceps, triceps, legs, his waist a little wide. A good friend.

Dave Draper-The Blond Bomber

One of my best friends, we use to call him the blonde bomber, tremendous back, good arms, small forearms, a very nice guy.

Robby Robinson-The Black Prince

Good physique, small calves, no forearms, good bicep peak, still around, and I hope he is still around for a long time.

Boyer Coe

Strong, good physique, something like Casey Viator.

Vince Gironda - The Guru

I met him after he had retired, good guy, he did not believe in squat, bench press, etc, I don't agree with all of his ideas, example with the squat.

Chris Dickerson

Good calves, strong. Too small, very good poser.

Bob Cajada

A nice small physique, small shoulders, not for international competition. Good for an amateur Mr. America.

Freddy Ortiz

Tremendous, you can't imagine what good arms, chest and back he had. No legs, or forearms, from Puerto Rico.

Tom Platz - The Golden Eagle

Strong, but his legs were too huge, probably the most famous legs in the sport.

Mike Katz

One of the biggest chests in bodybuilding. His chest was too big in proportion to the rest of his body. Great guy.

Bob Paris

A very nice symmetrical body.

Mohamad Makkaway

Too small, a symmetrical body, one of the greatest poser.

Mike Mentzer

Great, smart, massive, very strong, a legend in his own time.

Lee Haney

Good back, no forearms, good biceps and triceps, low chest, ok legs, no calves.

Flex Wheeler

Perfect. I like his body, it reminds me of my own body.

Ronnie Coleman

Potent, enormous, big, I don't like that kind of physique because then he has a big waist, like Dorian Yates, and small up calves.

Dorian Yates- The Shadow

Same as Ron Coleman, big waist.

Shawn Ray

I like his body, a well-balanced physique, good.

Jay Cutter

Massive, big, strong, I like his body.

Markus Ruhl

Too big, strong, not what I think a Mr.Olympia champion, should be.

Sergio Oliva

THE MYTH.

PERSONALLY SERGIO

What kind of restaurants do you like to eat at?
I like to eat at different restaurants; I like Italian, Greek, Cuban, and Mexican.

What kind of foods?
I like to eat different kinds of foods. I like to eat Italian pasta a lot.

Which sport do you like best?
Boxing and Baseball

Which baseball or football team do you like?
Not a specific one, because I like more than one.

Which is your favorite TV show?
I loved Threes Company it was my favorite, I enjoyed it a lot. In Spanish I like Viviana a la Media Noche.

Favorite singer?
I like Pavarotti a lot, in Spanish I like the queen, who just passed away, Celia Cruz, I also like Oscar De Leon, El Caballo de la Salsa (the salsa horse) who reminds me of the Great Cuban singer Benny More.

Special award on the job?
I received a medal of honor for saving the life of a man I once knew, I wrote about this incident somewhere else in this book.

Best gift?
The medallion and chain my late mother gave me.

Worse gift ever?
When they stole the Mr. Olympia title in 1970 and in 1972 and gave it to Arnold.

Favorite color?
Not any, just a good combination is enough for me.

What do you like to do in your free time?
Dance of course; I go dancing Fridays and Saturdays. I also like to play billiards, and I'm not too bad playing it.

What type of women do you like best, blondes or brunettes?
I prefer brunnetes but of course, I like blondes, too.

Where do you like to go on vacation?
I don't really go any place anymore because as you know, I have already been all over the world, I've been to South America, Central America, China even before Nixon went, Japan, all over Europe including Russia, Germany, but I don't really travel anymore except for doing special appearances. I like to stay around with friends and family. Bodybuilding has taken me all over the world.

BODYBUILDERS FROM A TO Z

Steve Reeves	Johnny Fuller
John Grimek	Bertil Box
Reg Park	Greg De Ferro
Bill Pearl	Mike Christian
Vince Gironda	Samier Bannout
Larry Scott	Mohamed Markway
Dave Draper	Lee Haney
Rick Wayne	Josup Wilkosz
Serge Nugret	Lee Labrada
Mike Katz	Tom Platz
Dennis Timerino	Chris Dickerson
Roy Callender	Dorian Yates
Lou Ferrigno	Lee Priest
Bill Grant	Flex Wheeler
Kal Szkalak	Shawn Ray
Arnold Schwarzenegger	Pall Dillet

BODYBUILDERS FROM A TO Z (CONT.)

Danny Padilla	Nasser El Sonbaty
Frank Zane	Markus Ruhl
Mike Mentzer	Ronnie Coleman
Robby Robinson	Bob Paris
Ed Corney	Kevin Levrone
Franco Columbu	Chris Cormier
Casey Viator	Jay Cutler
Albert Beckles	Jean-Pierre Fux
Boyer Coe	Mike Matarazzo
Ray Mentzer	Frank Marchante
Harold Poole	Leroy Colbert
Chuck Sipes	George Eiferman
Dan Lurie	Elmo Santiago
Clancy Ross	Reg Park
Jack Delinger	Chet Yorton
Marvin Eder	Armand Tanny
Reg Lewis	Fredy Ortiz
Irvin "Zabo" Koszewski	Eugen Sandow
Sigmund Klein	Victor Martinez

Mr. Olympia 2005

I was invited to be a judge for the new "Challenger Round" in the 2005 Mr. Olympia. All the judges were past Olympian champions such as Larry Scott, Frank Zane, Dorian Yates and Samir Bannout, etc. When the competition was over we all went up to the stage and were joined by Arnold and Weider. Weider was weak and had problems walking because of a back surgery he had.

After Arnold spoke, he asked me to come to the front to take group pictures with Weider and the guys. I said no thanks but he insisted and pulled me to the front.

Suddenly he grabbed Joe Weider's hand and placed it on mine. He then went to the other side and held Weider's other hand. Joe looked at me for a few seconds just as surprised and shocked, as I was.

I didn't want to do this but I didn't want to be rude with the fans and TV viewers. I imagine some people that were there probably realized how uncomfortable I was but that's the way it was. In general, however, it was nice and I enjoyed it.

I mingled with all the champions and enjoyed watching all of them. I had a nice time and many memories came to mind. I'm glad bodybuilders are making more money now, but we still need to make sure competitions are fair.

Titles and Competitions

People ask me often, Sergio which competition meant more to you? I can never answer that question. They all meant a lot to me, but you never forget the first time you win. The first time I won Mr. World, Mr. Universe and of course my first Mr. Olympia were the greatest. However, all of them meant a lot to me at that moment in time.

This question is the same as when somebody asks you which love meant the most in your life? They all meant a lot at specific times in your live.

Bodybuilding was and still is part of my life. I still read muscle magazines and enjoy

Courtesy: Robert Kennedy

competitions that I attend every year. Of course I keep training at World gym in Chicago every day for one or two hours not as hard as I use to though.

Going back to the question, the answer is I enjoyed every one of my competitions, win or lose they will always be a part of me.

Sergio Oliva's Best Measurements

Height: 5' 11" 1/2

Weight: 255 pounds

Chest: over 58 inches

Waist: 27 inches

Arms: 22 1\2 inches (cold)

Forearms: 20 inches

Thighs: 33 inches

Calves: 19 1\4 inches

Photo: Denie

TITLES WON:

1963 Mr. Young Chicagoland (1st)

1964 Mr. Illinois (1st)

1964 AAU Mr. America (7th)

1965 AAU Jr. Mr. America (2nd) + (Most Muscular)

1965 AAU Mr. America (4th) + (Most Muscular)

1966 AAU Jr. Mr. America (1st) + (Most Muscular)

1966 AAU Mr. America (2ND) + (Most Muscular)

1966 Mr. Olympia (2nd)

1966 IFBB Mr. World (1st)

1967 IFBB Mr. Universe (1st)

1967 IFBB Mr. Olympia (1st)

1968 IFBB Mr. Olympia (1st)

1969 IFBB Mr. Olympia (1st)

1971 Mr. Universe (2nd)

1972 Mr. Olympia (2nd)

1972 WBBG Mr. Galaxy (1st)

1973 WBBG Mr. Galaxy (1st)

1973 IFBB Pro Mr. International (1st)

1974 WBBG Mr. Azteca International (1st)

1975 WBBG Mr. Olympus (1st)

1976 WBBG Mr. Olympus (1st)

1977 WABBA Pro World Championships (1st)

1978 WBBG Mr. Olympus (1st)

1980 WABBA Pro World Cup (1st)

1980 WABBA Pro World Championships (1st)

1981 WABBA Pro World Cup (1st)

1984 WABBA Pro Mid-State (1st)

1984 IFFB Mr. Olympia (8th)

1985 IFBB Mr. Olympia (8th

Some Magazine Covers

1968 Peak Muscle Maker

1968 February IronMan

1968 March Muscle Builder

1968 June Mr. America

1968 December Muscle Training Illustrated

1969 March Muscle Builder

1970 June Muscle Builder

1978 January Bodybuilding World

1978 May Muscle Builder

1980 April Muscle Training Illustrated

1981 March Muscle Mag International

1981 Health and Strength

1985 February Body Power

1995 May IronMan

2000 May Exercise Protocol

Mag Covers

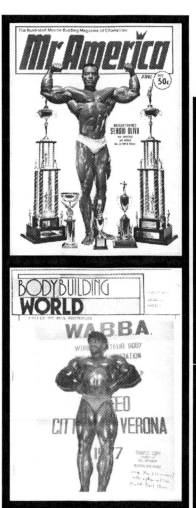

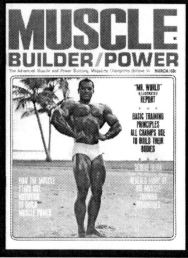

Mag Covers

Most Outstanding Prestigious Awards

Guinness World Record –Mr. Olympia 1968 Sergio competed/won unopposed.

WBBG inductee Sergio Oliva to the **"HALL OF FAME"** in 1977

IFBB inductee Sergio Oliva to the "**Bodybuilding Hall of Fame"** in 1999

IFBB voted Sergio Oliva as one of the top five throughout the world history of Bodybuilding in 2001.

Life Achievement Award in 2002

Outstanding Latin Sports Award in 2003

Lifetime Achievement Award from Flex Magazine 2004

MuscleMag International voted Sergio Oliva as one of the top five bodybuilders in the world.

The Cuban sport **"Hall of Fame"** inducted Sergio Oliva on Feb. 8, 2004

IFBB voted Sergio Oliva among the top 40 best arms throughout the world history of Bodybuilding in 2005.

Flex Magazine lists Sergio among the 20 most aesthetic physiques of all times in 2006.

Movie Career

One night a producer called me and told me he was sending me a travel ticket, $1, ooo dollars cash and all expenses paid to travel to Acapulco, Mexico to see if I wanted to take part in a movie. At that time, I was a Chicago Police Trainer and I called my Captain in the Police Department to tell him that I was going to take two weeks off. When I met the producer and talked for a while he stood up and told the rest of the producers you have to sign this champion, he is a natural actor. He told me, we don't want an actor from a school, we are looking for someone natural, like you, and you are a natural.

Black power movie poster –Hollywood

He said here is the contract, look it over, sign it, and we will give you a chauffer for two weeks while you think about it. Spending two weeks in one of the most exotic and beautiful beaches in the world was a lot of fun, I was young and in good shape. Many people recognized me in most of the places I went to and they wanted their pictures taken with me, my autograph or just say hi! Some women wanted to touch my biceps. I enjoyed walking down the streets and shaking people's hands, visiting the local outdoors market, the Mexican music, breathing and smelling the pure air from the beach, beautiful women walking by, left me with beautiful memories of my trip. I really enjoyed those days in Acapulco. I even went dancing to some of the most popular nightclubs of the city. The whole atmosphere was great, the music, the food, the sun, and the people were all very friendly. What a great time I had in Acapulco! I went back to Chicago, and requested two months leave from work to go back to Mexico with all expenses paid. I was also promised a percentage of the movie's profits.

I went back to Mexico and we flew to Venezuela to film the movie. The co-star was a very famous and beautiful actress Lydia Murillo, who was married to El Puma, a famous Latin singer throughout Spanish speaking countries. Another famous actor that worked in that movie was Mario Armada. The movie's name was "Black Power'. Black Power broke all the records in South and Latin America. After that one, we filmed "Los Temibles" (The dangerous ones) it was done in Durango, Mexico where John Wayne did a lot of his movies. It was very exciting and a lot of fun! I even had to ride a horse without a saddle. Gradually, more and more people recognized me and treated me like a celebrity. More people wanted to have their pictures taken with me or asked me for my autograph. Those days in Mexico were a very exciting and fun time in my life.

I was also offered a small part in one of Arnold's movie "Red Heat". I did not accept the role, because I believed it was a mediocre part for me, and if I had never lost to him in real life, why would I lose to him in a fictitious movie? No thanks.

Hollywood movie Premier "Black Power" Guest posing exhibitions and Seminar.

Bob Cajda

People are always asking me if Bob taught me. My answer to this is Bob is a great guy, and a great champion. When I started training at the Duncan YMCA he used to workout there. We became friends and trained together for a long time. He told me about competitions; soon I started to develop my own style of training.

I read articles from different muscle mags, as I learned English. With time and trial and errors, I discovered what made my body grow, cut, and define. Nobody taught me, I learned it by myself trying different approaches. This way I was able to find out what worked for me. But not necessarily worked for Bob or even you.

Bob was the one who told me "Why don't you compete, there is no one who could beat you professionally". I told him he was crazy. However, he was the one who gave me the idea. My first competition, Mr. Chicagoland, had a funny twist to it, when the judges would say turn right, I would turn left. Face back, I would do a double bicep and so on. I won that title without understanding English at all.

After the Mr. Chicago competition, Bob and I started getting ready for the Mr. Jr. America title. We both competed in weight lifting. I won 1st place and he got 2nd or 3rd in his class. Then I started to pump in the back to compete for the Jr. Mr. America and when I came out everybody in the audience could not believe it. I also won Jr. Mr. America that night, best arms, best legs, best chest, best everything except best abdominal. I took home a whole bunch of trophies that night. I was very happy.

Three weeks later Bob Hoffman was having the AAU Mr. America. Hoffman was known for not wanting any black athletes to win. In my opinion, he was a racist. Usually when you win Jr. Mr. America then you win Mr. America.

However, they gave the Mr. America title to Bob Cajda instead. Bob did not want to accept the title because he said that I deserved it. He said, "I don't feel right", I told him "Take it, and don't think about it, you are my friend." He is still my friend to this day. History has repeated itself again for this competition because I had won best legs, best arms, best chest, best everything except abdominals but I was not given the Mr. America title.

Cajda use to tell me "You will beat Larry Scott and all the others." so Bob introduced me to Joe Weider when I flew to New York for the Mr. World. At that time Weider was still new to competitions. I won Mr. World in 1966 and in 1966 I competed against Larry Scott for the Mr. Olympia. I got 4th place and Larry, one of Joe's favorite, retired.

Looking back, I can say that those were the good old times. Bob Cajda, is a great guy, and friend, whom I will always admire and respect.

Draper Buzz

SERGIO   BY DRAPER

Sergio Oliva literally broke the mold, and he broke it in more than one place. One might say he shattered the whole darn thing. After the man of cartoon-like dimensions came on the bodybuilding scene in the '60s, normal over-sized musclemen looked with both dazed eyes and vacant stares and said, "What's the point? Why bother? The bodybuilder from Mars has arrived."

Thankfully, I met Sergio after winning Mr. America and Mr. Universe, for me the two titles that meant anything in my un-extended competitive career. He could and would be beaten in a contest where subjective opinions were weighed, but who really looked like this creature for basic power, muscle size and density, hardness and symmetry? Another species of animal not yet categorized? He revealed and displayed more than anyone before and anyone since a primitive muscular completeness... and a carriage of grace to belie the brute-ness.

So much for the rugged landscape, the exterior; what about the man? I spent less time with Sergio than I would have liked, as we walked in different neighborhoods, he the street beats of Chicago as a cop and me the sandy beaches of California as a driftwood furniture maker. What we did share in common was obvious: muscles made our jobs easier. "Right what's wrong" and "fix what's broke" and "prevent problems" were identifying characteristics that surfaced in our distinctly separate lives.

All bodybuilders connect at some fine place; there's a bond that unites and, after the dispersal of initial hesitations, a brotherhood is evident, whoever they are and whenever and wherever they meet. Sergio and I won large titles one week in New York City and the world famous contest promoter and magazine publisher had set up a photo studio (free over-ripe bananas and tepid bottled water included) on the fifth floor of a grim industrial building in obscure and littered lower Manhattan. Ten of us, all champions, clogged the ancient textile ruins that once hired twelve-year-olds for small change, I guessed, to weave some man's fortune. I somehow sensed history repeating itself with larger, older, better-fed kids the subjects of exploitation, another man's fortune in the making.

"You guys," shouted the choreographer, director, taskmaster, caterer and provider of small change... the big bologna, "listen to me... put on more oil... pump up... don't get dirty from the trash on the floor... watch out for broken glass... no, there's no toilets... Jimmy, be sure you have film in your camera,

329

eh... geez, hurry, you guys, take your pictures so we can go home. I'll send your return-trip airfare when all the pictures come out and you all look great."

Oops. I was the first to flip out and cause enough commotion to stop all activity. Lights, camera, action ceased. I was not... how would you say it?.. cool, calm and collected... mature. I was frantic. No airfare meant, "Ha, I tricked you again." In thirty seconds I was dressed in oil-drenched jeans, one shoe on and one off, head sticking through a sleeve hole of my tank top, gagging and clawing for the only remaining century-old, open-shaft elevator in NYC that should be red-tagged by a city safety official. Threats of blood and lawsuits filled the hot, humid and otherwise silent air.

Above the storm, turmoil and hallucinations stood one calm soul... in a pair of bright red posing trunks the size of a band-aid. It was Sergio with a grin and confidence and big arms that pulled me persuasively from the rickety grip of the defunct cargo lift. "Dave, Dave, Dave..." he said, "you can't go. We'll get your money now." "I don't want it," I said like spoiled brat with principals all of a sudden. "It's not worth it, brother. Life's too short," insisted the wise policeman, serving and protecting. "And you can't get in that rusty, broken down, stinky birdcage without me and I'm not dressed for it. Besides, it's safer to jump."

The bad and the ugly and the unnecessary went on for an instant before dissolving in halted laughs and relief. Lights, camera and action... The conflict resolved along with my conclusion that this guy is a peacemaker, ten feet tall and growing. Trust him with my life.

David, Chet Norton and Sergio Courtesy of Dave Draper- *Photographer Unknown*

Chapter 9

End of an Era

It's late. I'm sitting in my home office doing some catch up work when the phone rings. I extend my arm and pick it up. The voice of my friend and Author, Frank Marchante tells me, "Sergio, Joe Weider sold the business, Weider is out. He sold to American Media Inc, owner of the National Inquire".

Shit, we kept quiet for a few seconds. I just couldn't believe it. Joe Weider had been a part of my bodybuilding career. I was speechless for a couple of minutes.

Joe Weider made what bodybuilding is today, this is very true. You can't talk about professional bodybuilding without talking about Joe.

I never thought that I would hear those words. Let's reflect back for a moment. Thirty five years ago or more I was the first one to take a stand against Joe Weider and his IFBB organization. I spoke about injustice and the way the competitions were held and often altered, and that cost me deadly. I was hurt monetarily and professionally. At that time there was no place to go, Joe owned everything. Now and a couple of years ago others have taken a stand and have criticized Joe or the IFBB, some that come to mind are, Mike Mentzer, Robby Robinson, Serge Nugret and lately Shawn Ray and others. The difference is that now there are other magazines and companies that you can go to. Then it was just Joe and only Joe, there was no place else to go.

The question that came to my mind was what will happen to all of Joe's magazines? What about all the contests? I asked myself many questions. The news shocked me and without any doubt, probably shocked the rest of the bodybuilding world for sure.

I hope that this new era brings new hope for the athlete bodybuilders. Like freedom of speech inside the organization, the right to compete in any competition sponsored by the IFBB or not. Joe Weider gave a lot to the bodybuilding world but he was also a **tyrant**, he controlled the athletes completely.

There is hope now, but inside of me there is also a little bit of nostalgia left. I was part of Weider publications. Let's hope for the best. It's time for the professional bodybuilder to be able to compete in competitions held by different organizations, endorse different products if he or she decides to. Share the ownership of his own pictures and most importantly raise his/her voice to be heard with no reprisal or be banded or suspended.

In reality it is hard to put into words what I felt at that moment. I was just shocked and surprised about the end of an era

PAST & PRESENT MEN'S BODYBUILDING & FITNESS MAGAZINES

MuscleMag International
Hard Core
Muscular Development
RX Muscle
Flex
Strength & Health
Ironman
Men's Health
Mr. America
Pump
Reps
Exercise Protocol

Muscle & Fitness
Powerhouse
Muscle Power
Planet Muscle
Muscle Digest
Natural Bodybuilding
Men's Fitness
Muscle Training Illustrated
Muscle Media
Testosterone
Maximum Fitness for Men

PAST & PRESENT FEMALE BODYBUILDING & FITNESS MAGAZINES

Oxygen
MS. Fitness
Woman Physique
World Muscle Fitness Hers
Fitness RX – Woman
Shape
Woman Physique World
Female Bodybuilding

*Influential Bodybuilding People

Robert Kennedy - Publisher, Executive Editor & Creative Art Director, Author, Writer, Photographer of Musclemag International. Publisher of Oxygen Magazine, American Curves, Reps Magazine and Maximum Fitness for Men.

Denie- Famous Bodybuilding Photographer, Author, Editor, and Writer. But most importantly, a hard working man that without any strings attached, diligently helped throughout this project and befriended my Author, Frank Marchante.

Lee Labrada - Owner, CEO, Labrada Nutrition, Author, Pro Champion.

Arthur Jones - Founder/retired Chairman of Nautilus Sport/Medical Industries Inc, Chairman Of Medex Corporation.

John Grimek - Passed Away on November 20, 1998, at the age of 88, Muscle Development Magazine. First editor, Writer, Pro bodybuilder champion

Nancy Lepotorrel - Editor in chief Oxygen (woman mag)

Sarah Wells - Musclemag International assistant editor.

Kerrie Lee Brown - American Health & Fitness Editor in Chief

Dan Duchaine - Passed away, Writer, very controversial person on bodybuilding. Published Underground Handbook

Bob Hoffman - Passed away, past owner of Strength & Health Magazine and The York Barbell Company, founder of Muscular Development Magazine, and the AUU bodybuilding federation.

Steve Blechman - Publisher, Editor in chief of Muscular Development magazine.

John Romano - Muscular Development Senior Editor

Mikael Cataveras - Editor Men's workout & exercise & health magazines

Wayne Demillia - Chairman IFBB pro division USA.

Johnny Fitness - Musclemag International Magazine, Editor in chief.

Vince Gironda - Passed away, The Iron Guru, had special controversial training ideas, Gym owner, trained many champions and movies stars. He also competed in the late 50's.

Joe Gold - Passed away, Founder of Gold's Gym

John Balik - Ironman magazine publisher & editorial director.

Stephen Holman - Ironman Magazine Editor in Chief.

Dick Jones - Musclemag International Magazine Associate Editor.

Jeff Everson - Planet Muscle Publisher, editor in chief

Dan Lurie - Founder The Dan Laurie Barbell Company published Muscle Training Illustrated magazine, from 1965 to1993. President of Word Bodybuilding Guild-WBBG.

Peter Mcgough - Flex Magazine Editor in Chief.

George Depirro - Managing editor for flex magazine

John Parrillo - A much known training expert.

Peary & Mabel Rader - Ironman magazine Founder

Russ Warner - Famous bodybuilder's photographer. Passed away on October 27, 2004, at age 87.

Ben Weider - IFBB president, founder of IFBB. Joe Weider's brother.

Betty Weider - Feature Editor Muscle & Fitness magazine, model and wife of Joe Weider.

Joe Weider - Owner of the Weider Barbell Company, past owner and founder, IFBB, publisher and editor of Muscle & Fitness Magazine, Flex magazine, men's fitness magazine and Hers women magazine.

David Pecker - Muscle& Fitness, President & Ceo, Joe Weider founder

Art Zeller - Famous muscles photographer.

George Tuner - Gym owner, training expert, author and bodybuilder.

Steve Blechaman - Fitness RX (women) Fitness RX (men's) Editor in chief.

Elyse & Steve Blechman - Fitness RX (women) Fitness (Men's) CEO publishers

Rees Morgan - Men's Health Editor

John Ville - Men's Health deputy editor

Rob Kemp - Men's Health Senior Staff Writer.

Michael Caruso - Men's journal editor in chief.

Hobart Rowland - Men's Edge editor.

Stanley R Harris - Exercise & Health publisher

Michael Catarevas - Exercise & Health editor in chief

Jim Heidenreich - Energy (women mag) publisher

John Cribbs - Hard Core Muscle editor in chief

Carolyn Bekkdahi - Hers (women mag) Joe Weider founder

Juan Antonio Sempere - Men's Health Espanol Director Editorial

Neevy Mador - Men's Fitness Managing Editor Joe Weider founder

Chen N. Low - Exercise For Men only, publisher & editor in chief

Chen N. Low - Natural Bodybuilding & Fitness Editor in Chief

Steve Downs - Natural Bodybuilding & Fitness Editorial Director

Bill Phillips - Muscle Media Magazine Executive Editor, Owner of EAS supplements.

Steve Speyrer – Bodybuilding Expert

*At the time of writing

Oliva also excels in pool tremendously

Sergio Today

I've lived in Chicago, Illinois for the past forty years. I worked for the police department and loved my job because I got to help a lot of people. I have three daughters and a son. Sergio is 21 years old and Julie 19 years old. The others are older. For the last ten years or more I have been a single parent. When it comes to my children, I try to give them as much as I can plus the kind of life I did not have as a child.

Now that I'm retired I would like to keep active and help this city that has given me so much, maybe by helping young kids in the YMCA.

I remember one day I went into my trophy room at home and it was packed. So I decided to donate some of my trophies to the kids at the YMCA, especially the poor ones. I thought it would be a great way for the kids to get some kind of recognition for playing the sports that they played such as basketball, baseball or whatever it may be. So I took off the name plates from my trophies and loaded the trophies into a truck and had them donated to the YMCA. This was my very own personal way of helping kids smile, keeping them motivated to stay in sports and away from drugs and stealing. I also hope to see bodybuilders having fair competitions, and allowing them to freely compete under any federation. Hopefully there will be less drugs and more fairness no matter the color of your skin, religion, or nationality. I will also of course keep reading about bodybuilding

Sergio's Office- The Myth signing fan letters

and attending bodybuilding competitions whenever possible and who knows maybe be a judge in a competition someday. I would also like to see my son and daughter grow up with an education, a profession they enjoy, and a family of their own.

At this time I'm very occupied with raising my son and daughter, the gym and other personal matters. I'm very happy with the live God has chosen for me. So if you are ever around Chicago stop by and say hello, in the mean time I'll be hitting the weights! YES! I'm still working out for about 1 1/2 to two hours a day depending how I feel that day and I'm planning to do so till God allows me to.

Reflections of My Life

Photo courtesy of R.Kennedy

When I reflect back on my life, there are so many things I have done and seen, important and famous people I have met. I have traveled to so many foreign countries. I have lived under communism, been behind the Iron Curtain in communist Russia, been to China, all over Europe, and of course, all over the United States of America.

I have played roles in movies, made special appearances in news programs, been featured in magazines all over the world, and in stages with screaming fans. I've even been shot twice on two different occasions. I have also competed against and have met the most famous and toughest competitors of bodybuilding.

I have met many friends, and met beautiful women of all races, religions, and ethnic backgrounds. I've bought the cars I wanted. There have been times when I've had a lot of money and times when I've been poor. I have been in love

My Special Toy

a couple of times and sometimes I have been hurt. I was blessed when I was able to bring my mother to the United States for a couple of months after not having seen her for thirty years.

Last but not least, what I love the most in my life, are my children, my beautiful daughter, Julie, and my son Sergio. They are my reason for living and what keeps me going. What else could a very poor kid who was born and raised in Cuba that went through very hard times with the Revolution 50 years ago could ask for? Looking back in my life, I don't need to create, add, or delete anything. I wouldn't change anything in my life even if I could.

Every time I look back I amaze myself, everything that has happened to me in my life, feels like I'm reading a script or watching a movie. Remembering my childhood sometimes makes me smile and sometimes it doesn't. How did a poor kid from an island, get to be one of the top bodybuilding champions and traveled all over the world? Was it fate or just my destiny?

Through the years I overcame many barriers. The sixties weren't easy for somebody like me. Sometimes I wonder how it would have been if I had been born in America. Or I had learned English when I was five or six years old. How far could I have gone? My life has been like a roller coaster, fast up and downs, but at the end I wouldn't change anything.

I love the live I lead, the live of Sergio Oliva.

Life Achievement Award

Steve Weinberger, Bev Francis & Mr.Universe, Mike Katz

Life Achievement Award - New York

Retirement Party

Sergio, Yvette, Son Sergio, Daughter Julie standing and friends

Memory Lane

Family Pictures

Julia and Sergio Jr.

Father and daughter enjoy a dance in Julia's 15th party

Sergio Jr. posing for daddy

Julia 2 and Sergio 5 years old

Julia's First Communion

Julia's graduation 14 years old

Sergio Jr. First Communion

Sergio 16 yrs old

Sergio's beloved mother and Julia 5 years old

With long time friend Jack

Jack Lalanne and Sergio attending a WBBG Dinner

Juanito's photo

withJulia

Puerto Rican Parade

With Sergio Jr.6 months old

With best friend, Jack

SPY – The New York Monthly

November 1991

Excerpt

When Worlds Collide

Chamberlain-Russel. Ali-Frazier. McEnroe-Connors. Yankees-Red Sox.
Through the history of professional sport, great rivalries have captured the
imagination of fans with the promise of an elite level of competition and almost
magical aura. Bodybuilding has also had its shares of match-ups that have
had fans sitting on the edge of their collective seats: Grimek-Reeves, Reeves-
Park, Scott-Poole. But one rivalry was so heated that its combatant's
supporters still argue to this day as to who was the better man: **Arnold
Schwarzenegger or Sergio Oliva.**

Rivals in the Making
By 1969 Arnold Schwarzenegger had been brought over the United States by
bodybuilding impresario JoeWeider to help him promote his fitness empire.
Times being what they were black athletes did not have the same market pull
as white athletes, and the fact that Sergio was from a communist country
(despite the fact that he had defected from Cuba and was living in Chicago)
made him that much less marketable. So Joe put Arnold on contract which
meant that he paid for his room and board in Venice, California so he could
train at Gold's Gym with the top American champions and his European skin
could soak up the California sun.

Round 4
But in 1972 would prove to be the biggest threat to Arnold's supremacy of the
bodybuilding world to date. Because back from the shadows would emerge a
new myth – bigger and more define than ever before.

In the two years since they last met Sergio made tremendous
improvements while working with Arthur Jones in Deland, Florida. Arthur was
an inventor and innovator in the world of bodybuilding and had some
revolutionary ideas concerning bodybuilding training that Sergio was willing to
try in his quest to regain the Mr. Olympia title.

The exact nature of those workouts may forever be in dispute but the end
result was 5'10, 240 pounds work of art.

Sergio came out of Deland bigger and far more defined than ever before and was primed to take on the reigning champion. When Arnold caught sight of Sergio backstage at the Olympia, held that year in Essen, Germany, he felt chills similar to those he experienced the first time he

encountered Oliva. Now, not only was Sergio as big as, if not bigger than, Arnold, but he was nearly as cut. His shoulders were broader than Arnold's, yet his waist was nearly six inches smaller.

The story goes that Arnold realized on that day, as he had in 1969, that he might have been the second – best bodybuilder on that stage. Yet Arnold was crowned the 1972 Mr. Olympia.

The Aftermath

Writer Irving Muchnick, in his 1991 SPY magazine article "Pimping Iron" quotes Joe Weider as admitting to associates back in 1970, "I put Sergio in the cover, I sell x magazines. I put Arnold in the cover, I sell 3x magazines".

So we all know what became of Arnold but what about Sergio? Sergio, convinced after 1972 that he could never get a fair shake from the IFBB, competed in just the IFBB 1973 Mr. International uncontested and then turned his back on Weider and company. For the next 10 years, he competed in the WBBG and WABBA organizations, routinely defeating a mixed bag of competitors.

After 1985 "the Myth" would become "the legend", retiring from competitive bodybuilding with an unblemished legacy. To this day the debate still rages as to who was the dominant bodybuilder Arnold or

Sergio. To the layman, Arnold is still king. But most bodybuilders are of the opinion that Sergio, by virtue of his superior natural structure, was the deserving winner of most, if not all, of the wars. Photos from the 1972 Olympia in Essen seemed to indicate that Sergio was denied his title that night.

So while Sergio may indeed have been the better bodybuilder in 1972 the real question that remains is: Who was better at their best, Arnold or Sergio? It may be too close to call, but we try...

Comparing Sergio and Arnold at their peaks is like comparing apples and... different apples. Despite being so different in overall shape, the two were nearly identical in the way they dominated their competition.

Chapter 10

Afterword

I have given you in this book what I know will provide you with the knowledge to build a powerful, strong, symmetrical, and lean body. At the same time I have shared my memories, lifetime experiences, victories, defeats, greatest moments in triumph, and the pain and struggles of my life which I was exposed to and cannot change.

I hope that this book not only changes your body but also opens your mind to new horizons. I hope that you've enjoyed reading it, as much as I did writing it. Maybe together we can change for the better the sport of bodybuilding. Who knows, maybe one of you, reading this book will be the next greatest champion.

Your friend,

Sergio Oliva
The Myth

Photo - Jules Freedmond

REFERENCES

I have included some references that were consulted while researching for this book.

American Dental Association

American Heart Association-www.amhrt.org

American Diabetes Association-www.Diabetes.org

American Holistic Medical Association

American Arthritis Foundation

American Nutritional Association

Life Extension Foundation-www.Lef.org

Medical journals online-www.freemedicaljournals.com

USDA nutrition data base-www.nal.usda.gov

Complete Guide to Vitamins, Minerals and herbs-ISBN-0158330046

Live Longer with Vitamins & Minerals- Dr. Earl Mindell-ISBN- 8979836520

Food Your Miracle Medicine-Jean Carper-ISBN-0060183217

Life Extension Companion-ISBN-044651277x

Nutrition for active lifestyles-Dr. Earl Mindell- ISBN-8314800300

The Nutrition Reporter-www.nutritionreporter.com

Total Fitness-30 Minutes –ISBN-0671802704

Growth Hormone-ISBN-1884820301

MEMORIES WEB SITES

Sandow
Historic photographs of early bodybuilders
www.Sandowmuseaum.com

The Exercise Archives- David Landau-Rare & Antique Photos
http://members.aol.com/exarchives

GMV Productions Ltd
Wayne Gallash
www.gmv.com.au

Resource Books

The Incredible Lou Ferrigno –ISBN-067428632

Building the Classic Physique- Steve Reeves-ISBN-1885096100

Hard Core Bodybuilding-A Scientific Approach-ISBN-0809254581

Arnold. The Education of a Bodybuilding-ISBN-0671797484

Brother Iron Sister Steel-Dave Draper ISBN-1931046654

Beef It –Robert Kennedy-ISBN-0806977604

Raw Muscle -Robert Kennedy-ISBN-0809244705

New Encyclopedia of Modern Bodybuilding-Arnold Schwarzenegger-ISBN-0684857219

Muscle Quest-Gerald Throne & Phil Embleton-ISBN-1552100243

MUSCLE MAGAZINE REFERENCES

MuscleMag International

Health & Fitness

Muscle Planet

Muscular Development

Flex Magazine

IronMan

Natural Bodybuilding

Exercise for Men Only

Bodybuilding Associations Web Sites

ANBC   American Natural Bodybuilding Conference-www.anbc.org

IFBB   International Federation of Bodybuilders-www.IFBB.com

NABBA   National Amateur Bodybuilding Association-www.nabs.com

NABF   North American Bodybuilding Federation-www.nabfusa.com

NPC   National Physique Committee-www.npcnewsonline.com

Internet Websites

Steve Speyrer –Pro-Champion
www.Classicanatomymagazine.com

Flex Wheeler-Pro- Champion
www.teamflex.com

Gay Cutler-Pro- Champion
www.jaycutler.com

Shawn Ray –Pro- Champion
www.shawnray.com

Amy Fadhli-Pro- Female Champion
www. afadhli.com

Lou Ferrigno-Pro -Champion
www.louferrigno.com

Sergio Oliva-Pro -Champion
www.Sergiooliva.com

Steve Reeves-Pro -Champion
www.stevereeves.com

Danny Padilla-Pro- Champion
www.originalgiantkiller.com

Ed Corney-Pro- Champion
www.edcorney.com

Lee Labrada-Pro -Champion
www.labrada.com

Robby Robinson-Pro- Champion
www.robbyrobinson.net

Grace Rivera -Pro Female-Champion
www.gracerivera.com

Lisa Brewer-Pro-Female- Champion
www.lisabrewer.com

Lisa Brewer Fitness Model
Photographer
www.lisabrewerphoto.com

John Hansen-Pro- Champion
www.naturalolympia.com

Frank Zane-Pro –Champion
www.Frankzane.com

Dave Draper-Pro- Champion
www.Davedraper.com

Casey Viator- Pro-Champion-
History's younger Mr. America
www.caseyviator.com

About the Authors

Photo Michelle Marchante

Frank Marchante has been an educator for 29 years in Miami, Florida. In 2000, he was also one of the 30 professors selected in North America to participate in the People to People Ambassador Program in the Delegation of Counselors and Technology Education to the Republic of China. His selection was based on his professional experience, credentials, and competency.

Marchante, a huge fan of the sport of bodybuilding became involved in bodybuilding in the Golden Era. Through his life, he has trained many young men in bodybuilding including his own son Frank Jr. who won 2nd place in a 2002 bodybuilding contest in Miami. He has owned a personal gym for the last 30 years.

While working on this project, he was the speaker and recipient of the "Hall of Fame" Award for Sergio Oliva on Feb. 2004 in Florida and the speaker who introduced Sergio Oliva at a South Florida Bodybuilding Championship in 2004.

His other passion is sport flying, composing music, reading, and traveling.

Sergio Oliva one of the greatest legends throughout bodybuilding history has appeared on multiple magazine covers worldwide and has been a guest on popular television shows. He's also been on TV commercials, played roles in movies, and conducted seminars all over the world. He holds 31 professional bodybuilding titles, including Mr. Universe, and three Mr. Olylmpia titles.

Originally from Cuba, Oliva resides in Chicago, Illinois and is retired from the Chicago Police Force.

Printed in the United States
74264LV00001B/139-156